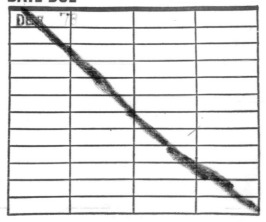

CONFRONTATION ON CAMPUS:
Student Challenge in California

CONFRONTATION ON CAMPUS:

Student Challenge in California

By ART SEIDENBAUM

Foreword by HARRY S. ASHMORE

PHOTOGRAPHS BY BILL BRIDGES

THE WARD RITCHIE PRESS • LOS ANGELES

To Kerry, Kyle and Jim
who were young enough to provide the motive
and
To Jim Bellows, Nick Williams, Jim Bassett
and Marshall Lumsden who were old enough
to provide the time.

Students were helpful wherever I went, even students who mistrusted me and my mission. Administrators and professors were generally helpful when asked. I tried not to ask often because this was to be a student-centered search.

Several people whose names do not elsewhere appear in this manuscript were extremely helpful. I'd like to name them by campus:

UC SANTA CRUZ: Paul Rosenstiel, Jerry Samuels, Nick Robertson, Maurice MacDonald, Susan Queary, Ann Griffin

SAN FERNANDO VALLEY STATE: Dr. Julian Nava, Tim Harris, Nancey Oatey, Nancy Torbeck, Benjamin Caraveo

POMONA COLLEGE: Hank Meyer, Dr. James Levy, George Sweeney, Mike Schulman, Eileen Wilson

UC SAN DIEGO: Dr. John Stewart, Chuck Champlin Jr., Michael Einbinder, Dr. Gabriel Jackson

USC: Dr. Joseph Boskin, Sam Hurst Jr., David Raksin, Dr. J. Wesley Robb, Dr. David Martin, Margaret Hallock, Jim Ansite, Stan Metzler

SAN FRANCISCO STATE: Dr. Barry A. Goodfield, Petra Fischer, Bill Better, Noni Garner, Dr. John Bunzel

STANFORD: Linda Thorne, Jeff Weil, Kathy Barrett, David Turner, Bob Beyers, Bob Freelan, Fred Lonsdale

UCLA: Gene Wilhelm, William Johnson, Larry Borok, Glen Leichman, Andrew Hamilton, Dr. Lee McEvoy, James Howard, Dr. Keith Berwick

UC BERKELEY: Peter Bailey, Barbara Cowan, Dr. John Bilorusky, Dr. Allen Cohen

CONTENTS

Foreword by
Harry S. Ashmore

E. B. White, who may be the most civilized American, turned seventy not long ago and exercised the anniversary privilege of recalling his college days. "Universities have become very big," he said, "and with bigness comes remoteness, inaccessibility. This is bad and it causes trouble. When I was an undergraduate, there were a few professors who went out of their way to befriend students. At the house of one of these men I felt more at home than I did in my own home with my own father and mother. I felt excited, instructed, accepted, influential and in a healthy condition."

It is now evident that the university of White's memory vanished from the American scene at least a generation ago. The reactions of the most relentlessly articulate of today's students are the exact reverse of those imprinted upon the budding essayist at Cornell in the early twenties; now the young proclaim themselves neglected, alienated, and powerless, and their excitement alternates with waves of depression. Neither they, nor the institutions they denounce, and sometimes assault, can be considered in a healthy condition.

Most observers would agree with White that bigness has a good deal to do with the malaise that has settled over the nation's campuses. California, where nearly a million students are enrolled in the world's most comprehensive system of higher education, has been in the vanguard of the spreading student revolt. Clark Kerr, the deposed head of the gigantic state apparatus, coined the term "multiversity" to describe it. The core of intimate, personalized instruction gratefully recalled by White presumably is still embedded in, or diffused through, a vast collection of colleges, graduate schools, research institutes, and service agencies looming in high rise on campuses scattered the length of a prodi-

1

gious commonwealth. But if so, many of the hairy and bangled youngsters who wander through these great enclaves no longer locate it.

Defenders of the system say that, even so, the multiversity is a triumph of utility and democracy, standing at the apex of a 58 billion dollar educational structure. Before student riots led to his ouster as president of Columbia University, Grayson Kirk described this enterprise as "the greatest growth industry in America," and there is no apparent slackening of the popular demand that has pushed educational expenditures into a close second place behind those for defense. In response the multiversity annually certifies as educated a steadily increasing proportion of the children of parents who were themselves denied access to higher learning by lack of means or by social sanction; thus it has become a major instrument of the upward mobility that is the essence of the American dream.

It is argued, too, that the technological revolution's demand for specialized knowledge and skills has upgraded university faculties, and certainly this is true if the measures are income and status. There is no doubt that the size and broadened functions of the multiversity bring together a range and diversity of intellectual talent unheard of in the small, sheltered academy of old. Thus, it is concluded, the quality of instruction available today is the highest in history, on the average at least, even though it may be somewhat diluted by the necessity of making learning available at wholesale to students who get no closer to their senior professors than the front row of a lecture hall.

All of which may very well be true. It still misses White's point. The profound changes in social and physical environment over these fifty years have not ameliorated, but have tended to exacerbate the raging of the glands that coincides with the student years, and makes coming of age a schizophrenic process. The end of innocence can be, and usually is, accompanied by shattering disillusionment, and it comes at a time when the human animal is responding to a compelling need for individual identity. Traditionally this is fulfilled by throwing off the real and imagined restraints of those who have dominated his life, i.e., the family, or what's left of it in this enlightened and mobile age. The terrible loneliness that accompanies the assertion of manhood brings on a frantic search for community, for the excitement of belonging to something new and vital to replace the security of the familiar.

2

College provided community in this sense for those in the upper strata of E. B. White's generation, and the one that followed. The act of admission, even to a jerkwater denominational college or one of the ivyless state universities, guaranteed a new identity. The student became a member of a small elite, self-consciously different from the world outside, subject, on the surface at least, only to its own highly ceremonial rules and traditions. Requirements of civility in personal conduct that would seem preposterous and degrading when imposed in the impersonality of the multiversity were reasonable enough in a place where a student knew most of his compatriots by name, and sometimes found himself swept along by spontaneous intimacy between generations engaged in a common enterprise. White felt not only instructed but accepted, and therefore influential, and so there was no onus in his temporarily inferior status as an apprentice among presumed masters of the craft he sought to learn. Administration and faculty exercised authority based on accepted custom, and in the usual case the student was well along toward graduation before he began to note that some of the practices that comforted him through his change of life were manifestly undemocratic and irrelevant to the university's professed purposes.

Such of today's students as arrive on campus burdened with the illusion that they are entering a special and even holy place are quickly disabused by circumstances, and by their contemporaries. The computer card which establishes a track through the academic maze does not provide identity but erases it. The most conspicuous veterans of the classes ahead then move in to assure the freshman that the elders who control the university regard him as a faceless automaton, and have no interest in providing intellectual fare relevant to his personal needs, or to those of the deteriorating society outside the walls.

At the most conformist of all the ages of man, the fashion of the day gives the student a choice of identifying with the self-proclaimed revolutionaries who have mounted a verbal assault on all the evils of the great world, or of making a more personalized protest by withdrawing from the corrupt culture and seeking solace in some variation on the mystique of love. A considerable majority of students, of course, adopt neither stance, but plug along in the usual way, going after the diploma that is their ticket of admission to the affluent society. But the rebels are the stylesetters, and the most phlegmatic of the student squares must be

3

touched in some degree by the passionate life-style that provides the major component of the generalized description of the university scene in the mass media.

○   ○   ○

In the 1968-69 school year Art Seidenbaum set out on assignment from the *Los Angeles Times* to take a look at the particulars of the student upheaval as it is manifest on the many-splendored campuses of California. He ranged from the sylvan environs of Leland Stanford's one-time farm at Palo Alto to the raw, factory-style spread of concrete parking lot that is the necessary adjunct to the classroom at San Fernando Valley State. Seidenbaum recognized the reality of the generation gap and respected it: "No middle-aged man of diminished hair and expanded belly can dress himself up in student stripes and pretend to parade in their army. But I could cross chronological lines to ask questions and try to appreciate how things look from the other side." The view, as set forth in this volume, has been translated into a sympathetic appraisal of a "struggle for men's minds increasingly physical and considerably less academic."

The contest is many-faceted, and inchoate to the point of virtually defying definition by those most passionately engaged in it. Sporadically, the putative revolution aims at the practices of the university itself. But here, insofar as the personal lives of the students are concerned, the famous battles have been won and liberation is an accomplished fact. There is hardly a vestige of *loco parentis* left on the California campuses. Co-educational dormitories with practically unlimited visiting privileges are not unusual, and those who want to avoid even these minimal inhibitions are free to assemble in commune-style apartments off campus. There are no effective rules, and no real social sanction, against liquor and drugs. Speech is free, commonly obscene, and virtually endless. The internal issues that still exist turn on academic matters of grades and courses, and those that can be, by sometimes tortured logic, related to the running controversies of the outside world: race, the draft, ROTC, armed forces recruiting, defense-oriented research, and the investment of endowment funds in ghetto property or armament manufacturers' stock.

A generation whose battlecry is "Now!" quickly wears out issues and leadership, and this imparts an inevitable faddishness to the

4

action. "I've found that every year I've been here there's been a theme," a student at UC Santa Cruz told Seidenbaum. "Two years ago it was drugs. Last year it was sex and love. Now it seems to be anarchism and violence, tied to the idea of black power."

The reaction at Santa Cruz is particularly significant, and profoundly discouraging to those who think there may be some simple, structural answer to the student rebellion. There, on lovely highlands overlooking Monterey Bay, the University of California has undertaken its most ambitious effort to recapture the vanished collegiate sense of community. Around a core of central facilities are clustered small, self-contained colleges so arranged as to guarantee sustained contact between students and teachers. The hubbub of the San Francisco Bay Area is far away across the mountains, the faculty is first-rate, the curricula are flexible, and the administrators hospitable to experimentation. But Seidenbaum's first casual encounter in this pastoral setting elicited a co-ed's resounding condemnation of her alma mater:

"My friend says to be a revolutionary, you not only have to have some sympathy for the oppressed, you've got to be a little oppressed yourself. Nobody is sufficiently oppressed to be a revolutionary around here. . . . The trouble at Cowell College is guilt. Guilt because we can't hate Page Smith, the provost. Because most of us are middle-class and because we still want a car to drive to San Francisco on weekends. Because there aren't more black students here. It was better the first year when the chancellor complained about public necking and dumb things like that."

There is some appreciation among the students of the irony of the rebel without a cause, but not as much as the older generation tends to expect. One of the few spokesmen of the young who has earned a reputation for his sense of humor has generalized the condition cited by the frustrated young lady at Santa Cruz. In a syndicated newspaper article, James Simon Kunen, who chronicled the Columbia rebellion in *The Strawberry Statement*, wrote of his plans for a trans-continental voyage of discovery:

"Driving offers freedom with security, hitching—freedom *from* security. I am going to hitch. I encounter some resentment when I mention hitching to people who know that I could afford to give other people rides rather than begging my own. . . . There it is. The new guilt of the New Left. No sooner have we bounced the old fears and guilts than we've shunted in our own. There is something in the air that makes one fear making money, even if it's incidental to legitimate liberated activity. There are new constraints. Is it wrong to hitch when I could buy a car? Is it wrong to buy a car from a big corporation? Is traveling and writing radical? I am perhaps being absorbed, co-opted, repressively tolerated. A house radical. An entertainer. There isn't any realm where you can just have a good time . . ."

◦   ◦   ◦

It will be seen that Kunen is laughing at himself, but not very heartily. Lack of humor, at least by adult standards, is one of the hallmarks of the student revolt, and it is perhaps inevitable in the nature of the case. "One of the major troubles with students," Seidenbaum found, "is that they're really afraid of being rejected even though they are the most knowing, most sophisticated, most vocal kids ever produced." A man acting out of his own basic insecurity is likely to be afraid of laughter, and if he couches his protest in terms of moral outrage he rejects the qualities of tolerance and good nature that are essential to spontaneous gaiety. Although it involves a good deal of self-conscious hedonism, the rebellion appears to an outsider to be a pretty grim business.

Perhaps because the university is its locale, and its method calls for automatic protest against any authority near at hand, the movement also appears to be determinedly anti-intellectual. There always have been those who, as the old radical, I. F. Stone, wrote of himself, "love learning and hate school." However, in this post-Freudian era some remarkable new twists have been added, and learning itself becomes the object of scorn. The campus revolutionary exalts the sensory as opposed to the rational, and at the extreme even claims that the revolutionary's dream of a New Man has come true through a process akin to osmosis: the great technological dislocations in communications and life-style that corrupted their parents somehow imparted to the young true insight into the human condition, and thus they come of age as members of a brand new revolutionary class, already on the far side of a radical disjuncture in the history of Western man.

It is probably impossible to tell how many of the young take this thesis seriously, and how many go along because, as Stone said of his own youthful anarchy, "it provides lofty reasons for

6

not doing homework." A recent Roper poll, commissioned by Standard Oil of New Jersey, which has some understandable curiosity about the attitudes of its future employes, undertook depth interviews of a national student sample and came up with this rating of major American institutions: 18 per cent very favorable, 48 per cent generally favorable, 25 per cent somewhat critical, and 9 per cent questioning the basic soundness of the system. But the Roper report adds: "This alienated minority has a significance beyond its numbers—for these severest critics differ only in degree from the more approving majority. The unresolved question is whether they are a spearhead of greater discontent to come or simply a sensitive index of current but temporary malaise."

I do not myself see any convincing evidence that the student movement is now, or could become, a genuine revolution. The more traditional radicals, the action-oriented leaders of Students for a Democratic Society, aim their activities off campus and assert that their immediate tactical need is to find allies among the genuinely oppressed—the blacks and the poor whites. But there is not really a proletariat in a country where the middle class embraces perhaps 80 per cent of the population. Most of those still on the outside, the ghetto blacks and the Appalachian whites, are mortally offended by the antic personal behavior of the youthful revolutionaries, and baffled by their doctrinaire preoccupation with such matters as the possible status of Ho Chi Minh as a bourgeois revisionist. And the students themselves frustrate their leaders as they vacillate between genuine moral concern for the community at large and their own conspicuous self-pity and self-indulgence, between dedicated support of unpopular causes and coltish horseplay. At Pomona, a leader of the crusade against ROTC confessed: "Most of us are still kids. Last night, on the eve of this major protest, we had a tremendous water fight in the dorm. There's still half an inch of water in the hall."

Seidenbaum found the rising generation characterized by an "astonishing abundance of candor, curiosity, social concern, self-concern, impatience, verbal style, and emotional confusion." These qualities were epitomized in his tape-recorded interview with David Graber, a 21-year-old Berkeley senior majoring in political theory:

"My own flirtation with SDS drives me crazy. I'll join every year, I'll go to meetings and I'll vote and I'll participate in things.

7

Then I'll quit because the people start to sound like mewling complainers . . . SDS parties are this intense interplay back and forth. The game, you know, who's the most radical? Who's gonna be liberal tonight so we can jump on him? You either make a mistake and say something liberal or you do it on purpose because you're feeling nasty and want to fight back. It's an exhausting thing. So I go in and then I pull out. Then I go in the woods and sit by brooks. This, other people do too—run away."

   ◦ ◦ ◦

Everywhere he went Seidenbaum found an astonishing and beguiling openness, an almost painful urge to talk about the most intimate doubts and fears. "I've got these heavy questions now," confided a long-haired freshman at Santa Cruz. "I'm very far to the left, but I'm also a coward, a physical coward. I was arrested once, at the Humphrey demonstration, dressed as a saint, and I only got out of it because I was white and middle-class and my parents cared enough."

These, of course, are doubts that have always plagued the young. Most members of the preceding generation settled the question of personal cowardice in one of the traditional rites of manhood and sources of community: armed combat. This student generation, with at least the passive consent of most of their elders, has rejected the initiation. They have condemned the tragic misadventure in Vietnam and their resistance has had a great deal to do with its ultimate winding down. But the distant war in some important ways may have wounded the well-to-do sybarites who stayed out of it even more grievously than it did the poor and the black who have done most of the fighting. The unresolved questions of manhood, and of moral right, may be sublimated in the frenetic action of protest, but they don't go away. Here's the saga of one student as caught by Seidenbaum's sympathetic ear:

"In the fall of 1967, I turned in my draft card—sort of on a whim. That was the period when there were a lot of us dropping out. We were going to save the world by showing we could live in hippie bliss. We had a house here in town. Pot. Sex. Love. We were evicted. We moved around . . . Some of us weren't in school during that time, but we were on campus all the time. Hell, we were heroes. I felt completely free after turning in my

8

card. Free, because the worst thing that could happen to me was going to happen to me—jail. That was a certainty. I could begin to enjoy myself."

But when the certainty did happen he and his companions discovered "we couldn't hack jail. If rehabilitation means obeying the law because you're afraid of cops, then I guess you could say I was rehabilitated at Santa Rita Rehabilitation Center." He then tried the retreat to Canada, but his conscience drove him back, and, unable to face jail again, he submitted to the draft, to enjoy the sweet irony of discovering that he was ineligible. So, with the threat of Vietnam finally exorcised, he has made his way back to the campus, and remarkably enough, has found self-fulfillment in the cool, intellectual labyrinth of mathematics. "I want to study and get the damn degree and not wash dishes," he says. But he adds: "I'm still hung up on the idea of participatory democracy. I really think that maybe, given a fair chance, neighborhoods can police and control themselves. You know, people do want to control their own lives. It's become a catch phrase. But it's a damn good catch phrase."

That may very well be the message the student generation is trying to get through to elders who themselves display a range of contradictory reactions that add up to emotional confusion at least equal to that of the young: permissiveness, youth-worship, prudishness, demands for repression in the name of law and order. In the perceptive articles collected in this volume Art Seidenbaum has made a considerable contribution to bridging the rhetorical gap between the generations. He proceeds on the assumption voiced by a Berkeley student· The radicals are no more screwed up than the rest of our society. This may not mark the beginning of a revolution, but it could mark the beginning of wisdom.

Center for the Study of Democratic Institutions
Santa Barbara, California
August, 1969

SANTA CRUZ:
Doubts in the Garden

I toured the fronts of higher learning in 1968-69, where the struggle for men's minds was increasingly physical and considerably less academic. I watched violent confrontations, heard astonishing confessions and survived the cultural shock of seeing students made into a mob. But there were other times, good times, when the undergraduates were almost at peace with themselves and with their world. And I was around as an ear from another generation.

No middle-aged man of diminished hair and expanded belly can dress himself up in student stripes and pretend to parade in their army. But I could cross chronological lines to ask questions and try to appreciate how things look from the other side.

That's why I went back to school. I sat in classes, stood at rallies, eavesdropped in cafeterias, copied down graffiti messages, drowsed at bull sessions and played wallflower at parties on more than nine California campuses. Always informal and unregistered; a kind of total audit of the undergraduate experience.

At UC Berkeley, I met a remarkable radical who swears dislike for other radicals because they are unable to read a proper wine list.

At Pomona College, there was an unforgettable evening at the Experimental Residence Project when two dozen beautiful students shared an exercise in body awareness with an interloping adult.

At San Fernando Valley State, boys and girls played guitar in the United Christian movement headquarters before turning themselves in at the Van Nuys jail.

At the University of Southern California, the student body president began the semester by listing 10 reasons a serious freshman might not receive a good education on that campus.

At Stanford, I discovered the silent radical, a young man who has burned his draft card without telling anyone and without joining any activist organization. When the time comes, he will go to prison quietly.

At UCLA a black student explained that she goes out of her way to be friendly to white students . . . just so whites will still feel wanted by somebody.

At UC San Diego, a boy insisted that the drug situation is under control; you don't see the speed freaks cavorting on the plaza until 2 a.m. . . . after they've finished studying for the night.

At San Francisco State, a student professing nonviolence hit a student demonstrator and then started to cry.

At UC Santa Cruz, a girl complained that the campus is full of unrest because there isn't enough campus unrest and students feel guilty about the tranquility. So let's start there, a campus with more tranquility than most.

Santa Cruz is one of the newest schools in the California chain, an experiment in humanizing higher education by returning to the Oxford idea of distinct small colleges within a mammoth university. More than an hour away from any major city, cooled by the clean wind off Monterey Bay, UC Santa Cruz creates its own community.

Students are respected citizens of that community. They are encouraged to develop individual courses of study. There are no letter grades assigned in the humanities or social sciences— pass/fail being the single standard. Undergraduates sit on committes with administrators and have a voting voice in college governance.

I drove up around the coast, beyond the drab slats of old mansions that have now become rooming houses, past the dead white stucco of the Dream Motel. The city of Santa Cruz is a resort that hibernates in winter, having nothing to do but wait for second-class summer vacationers who come by car and then ride roller coasters.

The living is almost ideal for students who want to room off campus. Rents are cheap. Landlords are relaxed. Even the police are benign. Kids call the town funky, referring to the creaky comforts of yesterday.

The university stretches across a plateau of rich meadow and redwood forest, above town and neighbors. The new build-

12

ings—simple plaster, strong concrete, heavy beams—squat beneath the treetops and do not challenge the natural skyline. The earth is soft, dark, ripe. I counted girls going barefoot to classes: about one in every four.

The path to the main library leads to a long wooden pedestrian bridge over a gorge in the forest and the walk to the dining hall is by a plaza that opens on the late sun, the grazing lands and a view of the ocean. In the courtyard between the administration offices and the classrooms sits a plain brown sack labeled, "Exchange Bag." The instructions are to take out whatever you want provided you replace it with something else. On a Monday morning, the bag already contains several discount coupons, a roll of undeveloped film, a half of a ham sandwich and a pair of red garters.

The students are not as pastoral as the place. The same cafeteria window that reflects sunset back to ocean has a pane reading "Kill the Pigs." The standard student costume is from the other bay area, a Berkeley collection of army fatigues, revolutionary beards and, for girls, loose serapes over loud tights.

One girl interrupted me while I was standing in the Cowell College plaza, making notes near the exchange bag. She wore green stockings covered by a floral print, surrounded by tablecloth lace.

"Awful, isn't it?"

"What?" I wondered, thinking she might mean her outfit.

"That," she said, pointing at the exchange bag. "This place."

Her hair walked down her back like a waterfall, her eyes were magnified by wire-rim glasses and the corners of her mouth smiled upward even while she talked.

"My friend says to be a revolutionary, you not only have to have some sympathy for the oppressed, you've got to be a little oppressed yourself. Nobody is sufficently oppressed to be a revolutionary around here. What are you doing anyway?"

I told her I was trying to figure out what students are doing.

"You mean sex, drugs, violence and all that stuff?" Obviously I was beginning to bore her. She yawned.

Well, I also want to talk to the silent majority, I said. And meet the students who don't join marches. I want to find out what they're really thinking.

"The silent majority exists only in speeches," she laughed and the wind pulled her hair around in front of her glasses. "First

13

of all, everybody talks. Second, they have opinions. The trouble at Cowell College is guilt. Guilt because we can't hate Page Smith, the provost. Because most of us are middle class and because we still want a car to drive to San Francisco on weekends. Because there aren't more black students here. It was better the first year when the chancellor complained about public necking and dumb things like that."

Nobody seemed to mind public necking in 1968. A Romeo in blond hair and blue jeans splashes pebbles at his girl friend's dorm window. She appears, looking smirky. She leans outside and they kiss. He says he has to study. She asks whether he's finished with her copy of Malcolm X's autobiography.

Peter Silten, a junior with sideburns longer than his nose, thinks the serenity is useful: "Santa Cruz is a fine place to grow up. Great deal of freedom here. Fantastic atmosphere. Faculty committed and involved. Very few people come from genuine families in this day and age. Very few people have any idea what a genuine community is—they've never experienced it. By experiencing it here, they're empowered to go out, take part, develop such communities for themselves in the future—even though we all know the outside world is not like Cowell College."

Advertisement on a community bulletin board just outside the student lounge: "If you are a serious flugelhornist we might be able to incorporate you into what may prove to be a most rewarding experience . . . We cannot tolerate one who treats his flugelhorn with anything less than devout reverence . . . A good flugelhornist is a frugal hornist."

A bona fide radical sits in the center of a massive wood sculpture on the Adlai Stevenson College plaza and frets about how to mount a meaningful protest in this benevolent atmosphere: "We had a meeting of people from several groups because we wanted to find an issue. The best thing anybody came up with was the prohibition against bare feet in the campus coffee shop. We actually began to evolve the tactics for liberation of feet when a couple of the most radical students laughed."

Demonstrations were postponed until Governor Ronald Reagan and the Board of Regents visited Santa Cruz. Reagan is an issue among students all over California. At Santa Cruz, the radicals called him dirty names and rocked the Regents' bus.

"Actually," continues the student in the sculpture, "it's confus-

Study in sculpture at Adlai Stevenson College Plaza

Sociologist Herman Blake, Cowell College's champion of black studies

ing to be for change in a brand new place. But if you think radicals are confused by Santa Cruz, then wait until you see The Garden, capital 'T', capital 'G'. Those kids are working their way back to something else."

The Garden is on a rise between two colleges, a rainbow rolling right along the ground. It began almost accidentally, at no cost to the taxpayers. A couple of years ago, a Shakespearean actor named Alan Chadwick stopped on campus to visit a faculty friend. He was charmed by the site, ran his fingers through the soil and decided it was the perfect place to practice his private passion: French organic horticulture.

Chadwick begged the school to let him plant on an unused patch of ground. He would furnish seeds, supplies, labor and, in return for growing rights, would offer free flowers and vegetables to the entire campus. The administration agreed; flowers could only ornament the image of a school at peace with its students.

Ecologically, The Garden is a blooming success. Each morning, near the main entrance to the campus, a kiosk brims with bouquets of everything in season, there for the picking. The vegetables are on call for any UCSC function, whether faculty meeting or formation of a radical student club.

Sociologically, The Garden raises problems. A few of the brightest students have become more interested in tending land than attending classes. Some have dropped out of school completely, leaving college but staying on campus. The Garden is now a threat to the very institution that made room for it.

"It becomes a kind of a trip," smiles Peter Jorris, who takes care of the herbs and is still a student. "People have to run back to The Garden for security and once you get involved, the place consumes you. We seem to be in direct opposition to everything about a university—the classrooms, the arguments, the pedantry, everybody talking without seeing or hearing the other person. That all seems so futile up here."

Chadwick's sub-community includes a shack where young gardeners can cook their own meals and a cluster of great redwoods which students like to sleep under when the campus police leave them alone. It is the magical place, to occupy the hands, satisfy the heart and take refuge from the printed page. Peter Jorris and friends talk about finding freedom at last.

Maybe. But authority also grows there. Chadwick walks around

17

his province bare to the waist, bellowing orders with beautiful diction, as if he were Caesar himself. No contemporary parent or dean dares cut such a despotic figure. The Garden is a warm bed of discipline, run by a stern horticulturist, staffed by a bunch of young people who unquestioningly obey. The Garden is a limited universe with its own organic historic certainty; that's more than the modern humanities can promise.

Humanist Maurice Natanson, professor of philosophy, tells his class in phenomenology that there are no young geniuses in this field. A philosopher reconstructs human experience and nobody can do that without years of prior study, years of learning what previous philosophies were about. Child geniuses? In math or music, yes. Not in philosophy.

"Oh wow," mutters a boy near the back of the classroom. He shakes his head and doodles variations of the ankh, the ancient Egyptian symbol for life.

Mary Holmes teaches The Ancient World in the vinyl brightness of a girls' dormitory and the message is mildly terrifying: "Do you realize what age your old age will be? Thirty-five. You'll be retired then with 60 more years to fill." A girl winces and then stares down at her bosom, as if to see whether the withering process has already started.

"We live at the end of everything," continues art historian Mary Holmes, curling a finger in her own white hair for emphasis. "The end of Western Civilization, the end of Eastern Civilization, the end of the Agricultural-Industrial Revolution. So we stand where no one else has stood and it's absolutely the most painful position to be in."

Psychologist Bert Kaplan runs a course called Interpretation of Personal Documents. "Yours is a new generation," he reminds them, clearly giving students the responsibility. "The ethic is to be open and not embarrassed." He calls a girl to the front of the lecture hall and bends toward her so that his nose is close enough to cross her eyes. "Now tell me your feelings," says Kaplan.

"Confusion. I experience almost a physical rejection of your nearness," answers the girl. She pauses to regain poise. "Not you exactly. But your proximity."

18

The newest faculty hero at Santa Cruz is Norman O. Brown, who is to undergraduate mysticism what UC San Diego's Herbert Marcuse is to undergraduate revolution. In his Myth and History course, Brown urges the students to "subordinate the tongue to the eye," to create a new language by speaking from their total beings and not their minds.

A girl squirms next to me in the lecture hall. She turns to the slumping boy on the other side of her: "Life is hell, not so much from evil as from neglect." The boy looks at her as if Norman Brown and she were conspiring to multiply his insecurities.

"See that guy over there," she goes on, indicating a student whose beard circles his face in gorilla style, "I knew him when he was shaved and super-straight. Like I doubled with him to a prom and then I saw him the other day and I said, 'Remember me?' And he said, 'Barbara.' And I said, 'Yeah, we did a lot of things together.' And he said, 'Fuck off' . . . and I thought he was a friend."

Uncertainty is the campus constant.

Jed Horovitz is a freshman transfer from UCLA, a widesmiling, Prince Valiant-cut blond who has tried schools and psychedelics and demonstrations in search of himself: "I've got these heavy questions now. I'm very far to the left but I'm also a coward, a physical coward. I was arrested once, at the Humphrey demonstration, dressed as a saint, and I only got out of it because I was white and middle class and my parents cared enough. Now, when I see a policeman, I make a point to ask the time or directions."

Having put down drugs and marches, Jed now searches for courses that will tell him what to do with his life: "I'm looking for something that suits me, not something I suit. Can you understand that? Does it sound wrong?"

Several searchers squat in the corridor outside Herman Blake's office, facing rows of students waiting. Blake is the only black faculty member at Cowell, an idea-brimming, free-talking bear of a man who wears *dashikis* and knew Malcolm X.

Some squatters want help with their independent study projects. Others want orders in the struggle, the same way student gardeners want orders in organic horticulture. There's a push to establish a new college at Santa Cruz named after Malcolm, dedicated to the study of black awareness. At least black people seem to know what they want, and that attracts uncertain whites.

"What many of these kids really want," says Blake, "is a vicarious existence." They want to know what it is to be black. He can't give that to them but he does make them feel better because there is this man in this office where they can take their guilt and toss it on the desk.

Blackness has become this year's issue at most campuses. Peter Silten tried to put it in a Santa Cruz perspective: "I've found that every year I've been here there's been a theme. Two years ago it was drugs. Last year it was sex and love. Now it seems to be anarchism and violence, tied to the idea of black power."

The Catalyst coffee house, in what passes for downtown Santa Cruz, is where campus activists often meet with the outside community. The place features peeling paint and hard-back chairs, a decor left over from the days when the city was swank and this was the swank hotel dining room. The sourdough bread is fresh and the pastrami is digestible. A veteran of the movement swills down his sandwich with ginger beer and confesses how a revolutionary changes into a math major.

He doesn't want his name used because he doesn't want to have further dealings with his draft board—it has already changed his life.

"I was here in 1965 when Santa Cruz opened," he begins. "The following spring I quit studying. I came back the next year, quit again the year after that. I didn't really want to be a student, you know, all the clichés about it not being relevant. Also a whole lot of it had to do with the draft.

"In the fall of 1967, I turned in my card sort of on whim. That was the period when there were a lot of us dropping out. We were going to save the world by showing we could live in hippie bliss. We had a house here in town. Pot. Sex. Love. We were evicted. We moved around.

"The Resistance at Santa Cruz was always more concerned with humanistic questions than military questions. Some of us weren't in school during that time, but we were on campus all the time. Hell, we were heroes.

"I felt completely free after turning in my card. Free, because

20

the worst thing that could happen to me was going to happen to me—jail. That was a certainty. I could begin to enjoy myself."

The sense of freedom persisted until a few Santa Cruz resisters decided it would be interesting to sample prison on a short-term basis before committing to the full sentence for draft evasion. They went up to Oakland to participate in a disturbance at the induction center.

"By random bad luck," he remembers, "some of us got stuck in solitary. We weren't the leaders or anything. It just happened. The jail sort of overflowed there were so many people arrested. That experience, really brutal, really insane, convinced us that we couldn't hack jail. If rehabilitation means obeying the law because you're afraid of the cops, then I guess you can say I was rehabilitated at Santa Rita Rehabilitation Center."

Several of his friends fled to Canada. He tried to follow them to Vancouver but the Canadians had a record of his Oakland arrest at the British Columbia border. So he hitched his way east and entered near Toronto.

"While I was riding back across Canada to join the others, I heard the Mounties were searching our house for dope. It was a bad scene, even there."

He was unwilling to brazen it out in Canada and unable to face the prospect of prison. So he finally submitted to an army physical and was classified 1-Y, meaning currently unqualified for service. "Now, for the first time, I could go back to school because I wasn't worried about the draft. I'm cynical about the possibility of a university teaching you what it's like to be a human being. But now I discovered I can enjoy math in and of itself.

"I want to study and get the damn degree and not wash dishes. I guess I'm still a radical up here," he smiles, touching his un-combed head. "But school isn't the place, you know. Radical social change doesn't mean more professors, doesn't mean a black studies program, doesn't mean letting Eldridge Cleaver speak. Radical social change means the redistribution of power and a university can't do that.

"This university, in particular, is in no position to do that. The radical activist knows the system is evil and that its continuing day-to-day operation includes horrific viscousness, dreadful vio-lence against people. Its normal everyday functions are part of that violence. But the activist knows that his constituency can't

21

see it in Santa Cruz, can't react to the everyday horror. That's why he goes out, at places like Chicago or Oakland, to provoke the kind of brutality everybody can understand.

"I'm still hung up on the idea of participatory democracy. I really think that, maybe given a fair chance, neighborhoods can police and control themselves. You know," he says, wiping the mustard off his beard, "people do want to control their own lives. It's become a catch phrase. But it's a damn good catch phrase."

Two bell-bottomed boys stand around the Cowell fountain in the late afternoon: "What do you want out of this world, man? *Karma? Satori?*"

"Naw," answers his friend, "just $100 a week for life."

On Thursday nights Cowell College has its student-faculty dinner. The kids dress for the affair, even if that only means throwing a tie and a suede jacket over jeans.

Most of the students seem to be the younger ones; almost all the juniors and seniors live in town and few of them return for the community function. Even after students had won battles over what Santa Cruz awkwardly calls intervisitation—boys and girls allowed in each other's rooms—undergraduates prefer to make their own homes off the grounds.

Part of the search is leaving parents and institutional substitutes for parents. Moving away from a residential campus is not just to make studying easier—or even make sex easier. It has more to do with finding oneself.

The program for this week's dinner is the Cowell Trio, one faculty member and two other chamber music professionals. They are good, but only half of the audience seems to care. Several boys are sleeping quietly, still in their chairs. Others start to drift out of the dining hall, careful to move between movements.

After the concert, some people dribble over to the vending machine room where there are devices that belch coffee and Cokes and Salems and noodle soup and tuna sandwiches and ice cream and candy and even change. But it is a uniform and sterile place. Each machine looks like another, and any one, in turn, looks like all the other machines in schools across this country. And they all look like computer centers.

A boy and a girl discuss whether they should hitch out of town for the weekend.

22

"Nobody stays here on Saturday," explains a young man stretched out on the cold floor. "In fact, I don't know anybody on any campus who stays around on the weekend except at Berkeley. Usually we go to San Francisco. It's nearer. About half of us come from L.A., which we hate. Vacation comes and the people who have to go back to L.A. get nauseous."

I was not nauseated coming back to Los Angeles; I suppose that's another function of age and acceptance and hope—the ability to keep your stomach separate from your dreams.

But I was also pleased with the people I met on the campus. They have an incredible ability to tell you what ails them, without any of our adult apologies or mature excuses. The math major, for instance, can say that he's afraid, can admit that he ran off to Canada, can allow that even running was more difficult than he figured. So he finally did the legal thing, took his physical and flunked. Safe at last. No credit to him. But he knows that, too. He exposes it flat out—no self-serving adjectives.

Jed can say "I accept the fact that I'm only human and only 18 and even if I'm better than other people, I'm only that." Didn't we all have those romantic, secret, outrageous explosions of ego? Yes, but we didn't admit them. And so we went on teasing our internal selves while we humbled our external selves to please polite society. I think the search has to go better when you can wave your hangups in the breeze for everybody to see.

Santa Cruz's obvious advantage is its once-removal from the streets and big-town politics and the older wings of the multiversity. That's also its contradictory weakness when you understand the guilt that students walk around with as if it were a formal assignment.

The outside world will saturate Santa Cruz soon enough, as the university grows toward an enrollment of 27,500 students. Distance offers little insulation these days. School loyalties are much less important than loyalties to causes, to contemporaries. Traditional athletic rivalries don't mean much. New intellectual battles, slicing across campus boundaries, do matter. The question is not which university you belong to, but which movement.

Gross numbers count. Sociologists, the indefatigable national nose counters, say that two percent of a campus normally comprises the activist leadership. At a large school such as San Francisco State, two percent means 360 able student bodies. At young

23

Santa Cruz, two percent translates as less than 50. That's important.

While 360 angry young men can effectively close a campus, 50 of them spread over four colleges and 2,000 acres can be lost in a redwood grove.

Santa Cruz's present small enrollment helps make it comparatively tranquil. The adults also help, a collection of teachers and administrators who really do care about responding to student aspirations. Santa Cruz tries to be attuned to the confused human beings it serves. The students are certain of that much.

VALLEY STATE:
Looking for the
Silent Majority

Going to San Fernando Valley State College is like going to a
regular job. It's just before 9 a.m. and thousands of us are in
the traffic pattern groaning and braking along Nordhoff Street.
At Darby Avenue, the cars swing right as if beaded on a string
and now everyone brakes again and inches forward and waits
for his turn at the automated entry gates.

I'm a vistor, which allows me to swerve around the Darby
line and drive up to the manned booth where a student employee
will provide a free parking permit. Strange world; we always
treat visitors better than the people who belong.

Young men and women run from their cars to the classroom
buildings, just as though they had clocks to punch. I catch up
to one boy with weeping willow sideburns and ask him whether
it's always this hectic.

"You should be here when it rains," he says, slowing to a fast
walk. "It's worse. The place gets flooded, brakes go out, kids are
splashed and we might as well have the Coast Guard handing
out tickets instead of the Highway Patrol."

He runs ahead. But up walks another student who sees me
taking notes, and asks if he can help. I tell him I am trying to
learn about his school.

"This college is in the middle of this nothing," he says, swinging
a green book bag in a wide arc to describe the territory. "Most
of us are from around here. We think what we live is a reality,
locked up in our houses and our cars. Cars are a big issue at
Valley because there's no more parking room. Forget expanding
educational opportunity; commuting is what counts."

He points toward a George Rickey sculpture near the main

entrance to the school. "Stop there," he says; "it's the most human thing you'll see on the whole campus."

The sculpture is a cluster of long steel arms that wheel with the wind, attached to a towering center support. It stands between the herringbone patterns of parking lots and a series of buildings that might make up an industrial park. The boy with the book bag has a point. The whole San Fernando Valley is a bland jam of suburban communities spread over a waffle-grid of streets, rising to an occasional factory or shopping center.

San Fernando Valley State College, the principal institution of higher learning in these parts, suits the neighborhood. It looks commercial.

But my first visit fooled me. I came to school in November, 1968, only two days after a major sit-in, and wandered around looking for scars or signs of more trouble. Valley State seemed perfectly peaceful, as if nothing radical had happened—or would happen.

At noon, the Sigma Chi's and the SAE's were demolishing their touch football rivals on two adjoining intramural playing fields. Both fraternities attracted loud followings along the sidelines. A gamin-faced, blond-haired girl was yelling, "kill, kill," each time an SAE end with a Mark Twain moustache caught a forward pass.

I walked a concrete path about three blocks to the open forum in the center of campus. The speaker of the day was a young man dressed like a CPA and hawking a privately-sponsored course in speed reading. There were only 40 students sitting in the square of benches; less than 10 of them seemed to be listening.

Two girls sat eating sandwiches and talking, ignoring the speed-read pitchman. "My mother keeps telling me," said the girl in an orange pants suit, "that once I get my degree I can be independent for the rest of my life."

"Sure," answered her friend, wiping her long black hair out of a tuna sandwich, "just buy PhD insurance and you'll be all right."

I did see one patrol car creeping along the interior roadway; no part of Valley State is completely protected from the automobile. But this campus policeman looked to be as neutral as the custodian riding behind a mammoth Clarke sweeper, a vacuum device larger than a man.

Order and cleanliness, those were their jobs. And that day the

26

Rally at Valley State; (now-shaved) student president, Larry Labovitz, at microphone

Noon BSU rally at Valley State

BSU leaders stroll Valley State campus

policeman and the custodian certainly seemed to be employed at an orderly place. Even the baby trees, dwarfed by concrete and structure, didn't shed.

On another day, after more than 40 students had been arrested for participating in the Black Student Union sit-in, the atmosphere was entirely different.

Noon. At least 500 students are crowded on the open forum benches and on the center lawn. This is a historic day on campus: for the first time since the occupation of the school's administration building, the Black Students Union is taking its case to the whole student body.

Teresa Tolliver, a pretty girl in a lavender dress, is the first BSU speaker: "In looking over the audience today, I see a group of white people out here. And I'm surrounded . . . I'm not prepared for a speech, so all I can do is speak from my heart . . . I came to this school in good faith and I did not know what racism really was until I came to this school . . . I didn't have any hatred in my heart for white people . . . Now what I felt upon entering San Fernando Valley State College was isolation. Because I am alone here. And being here as a black student sets me apart."

A few of the white students in the audience look surprised. But I overhear a boy standing near me tell his girl friend that although it's not so bad on campus, black kids are often treated like intruders when they go into town for a hamburger, or they're hassled by police just for being on the streets.

Almost all the new black students live on campus, in Northridge Hall. Unlike the majority, they don't commute.

Bill Burwell, tall and muscular, in black sweater, beard and dark glasses, speaks next. He would later emerge as a chief negotiator in the administration-student agreement to increase black and brown enrollments, expand ethnic studies at the school. But today he is offering a militant's lesson in history: "White power has been arbitrarily imposed on black people for four-hundred-and-some-odd years in this country . . . In the past, for the most part, the response has been one of accommodation. Black people have tried to adapt themselves to the tentacles of white power.

"I stand here today to say to you on behalf of the Black Students Union in this college and the Black Students Unions all over this nation, that we will no longer use accommodation. Now we are

determined that we will deal with you in the way you understand—and that is through open revolt."

Archie Chatman, who quit the Valley football team and charged
the athletic department with racism, winds up the rally questioning the goodwill of the whole nation: "If our country was so
concerned about human life, we would empty our grain bins and
feed all the starving people, instead of putting surplus food in
grain bins merely to uphold the price of wheat or to uphold the
price of eggs."

The crowd applauds and Chatman shouts, "That's right. We
would have our farmers utilizing the land instead of paying them
for *not* plowing . . . We are depriving people of the right to
exist in a humane manner. We have all of these foundations caring
for people overseas. We try to spread democracy. What we are
doing—we are spreading cancer. We are like a leprous, syphilitic
old man and we are spreading our syphilis throughout the world."

The applause is louder and clapping starts to roll in rhythmic
waves as Chatman calls for change in America, change in communities, change on this campus. He finishes and the audience, which
has grown to more than 600 students, stands to cheer.

A group of 19 radical leaders—black, brown and white students
who were arrested after the BSU sit-in—pick up a 50-foot chain
made out of pastel paper and put their wrists through its links.
They start a march toward the Administration Building, bound
to each other in a line. Half of the rally crowd follows them.
So do 10 faculty members.

No singing, no shouting, no talking. Just a silent ribbon of
people.

I can see nervous faces appear in the upper windows of the
Administration Building. Obviously some of those people are
afraid of being locked in again.

But the marchers stop at the large glass doors and the leaders
form a circle, raising their arms. "The chains of fear and oppression shall hold us no more," yells a black student, breaking the
silence and ripping his paper handcuffs. The other leaders drop
shreds of their broken chains in front of the doors, a symbolic
declaration of freedom.

The demonstration is done and students slowly start back for
their afternoon classes. But something has happened. The rally
moved a mass of people across this orderly campus.

Walking in front of me toward the library, two boys discuss the event.

"That's what you call a peaceful confrontation," says one of them.

"That's the only reason I joined it," says the second, a boy with hair short enough to pass military inspection. "I'm with them when it comes to marching and I wanted the college administration to know it."

A science student, wearing a white button-down shirt and laced-up shoes, explains that he and many of his friends have been for and have been against the radical students.

"It depends," he says. "For instance, I was really happy when the BSU took over the building. Finally somebody was busting down some of the walls around here. I was even glad when the SDS followed the black kids and occupied another floor."

We're sitting having coffee at the best place to sit on campus, the roof of Sierra Hall. It overlooks the other buildings and the parking lots and—on a smogless day such as this one—we can see the corrugated natural skyline of the Santa Monica Mountains.

"I turned off the revolutionaries," continues the student, "when I heard there were kids threatening people. I'm still anti-violence. But then when so many kids got busted, some of them not even the right kids, I switched again. I'll probably keep switching as long as I figure the complaints are just, which I do, but I don't think the tactics always are. Hey, have you met Larry Labovitz?"

I admit I haven't.

"You should. The funny thing about this place is we're beginning to get some anti-revolutionary kids who are as wild as the radicals."

Larry Labovitz is delighted to be interviewed. We meet in the main cafeteria, a space so crowded in early afternoon that, near us, a boy who wants to study plunks himself down next to a couple who are kissing.

Larry Labovitz looks like a radical. He sported a Zapata mustache and goggle-sized glasses. And when this 22-year-old history senior starts to talk across the table, his voice is at platform pitch, full of the passion of a man running for something. Labovitz collected 2,000 Valley State signatures on a petition condemning

31

violence and supporting the administration after the sit-in. Now he is threatened for his troubles:

"You couldn't believe how vilified I've been in the last few weeks. I've been accused of being Wallace's best friend, Lenin's best friend, Rafferty's best friend. Actually, I'm a poor Jew who lives in the borscht belt of Los Angeles, tired of hearing all this crap."

Labovitz is convinced that white radicals hate him, black radicals hate him and the campus newspaper hates him: "My petition was the biggest spontaneous thing that's ever happened here and every radio or TV station, every newspaper in town covered it. But the *Sundial,* our own daily, couldn't send a photographer. The campus paper refuses to admit that I have relevance.

"I was attacked verbally for one hour before I came to meet you—by the SDS— because I wasn't doing the true activist thing and flunking my classes. A few members of SDS and a couple of BSU don't want an education; they only want to destroy. And so they work 24 hours a day at that.

"My hassle is that I want to stay in school, graduate, and still fight them. I never was an activist before—I never felt threatened before. I don't object to what the BSU demands. I tell them, if you can get it now, beautiful. But if you're gonna walk on my face, then I'll fight you."

Labovitz is a founder of a new statewide newspaper called *Open Campus,* which is his answer to the *Sundial* and the underground press. He claims the paper gives voice to the so-called silent majority, although Labovitz also admits that student opinion keeps changing and majorities move and shift, depending upon the specific issue.

"I'm mainly told that my whole involvement is an ego trip," Larry says. "Well, I admit my ego is pretty heavy but it has to be if you're going to organize, if you're going to try to give other students the guts to find a decent position. My real purpose is to end campus apathy, make people think. There have to be other voices here besides the New Left." Labovitz is often called a conservative at Valley State. That's an interesting label for a young man who registered for the Peace and Freedom Party in his first Presidential election year. It suggests something of a definition gap that exists between the campus world and the outside world.

Although he is student body President for 1969-70 Larry Labovitz

32

has reason to feel lonely here. Because he is indeed an activist and many of his political allies are not yet committed to action. He has little day-to-day support out on the quadrangles and if that makes him slightly suspicious, it's understandable. "You know I'm never Larry Labovitz to the New Left," he complains. "I'm not even *that* Labovitz. I'm always that fucking Larry Labovitz."

An astonishing student named Avrum Fried is one of the New Left antagonists, a brilliant 6th semester sophomore who keeps dropping out and then coming back and signing up for stimulating courses that do not advance his class standing. On the side, Fried claims to be a minister of defense for four organizations: the local SDS, the regional Student Abortion Society, the Southern California chapter of the International Werewolves Society and the national Up-Against-the-Wall Motherfuckers group.

The electric-haired Avrum Fried, with all his titles, is gentle in behavior, perfectly timed in delivery and merciless in dialogue: "I told Labovitz that if he kept getting that petition signed, then he'd never get laid. You can tell he hasn't made love lately by his crummy masturbatory political position."

I wondered about the sit-in; did taking over a building ever really accomplish anything?

"Of course it was stupid," says Fried, imitating establishment anger. "It was the dumbest, least practical thing I've ever seen in my life." He hesitates long enough to assume a saintly expression. "And it was beautiful. What else do you do with a society when none of the channels work?"

Any school where Avrum Fried wants to keep learning can't be all touch football. And any school willing to keep teaching Avrum Fried can't be all oppression.

One of Avrum's defenders is Tom Lasswell, a young Presbyterian minister who works with the United Christian Movement and has office space in the Jewish Hillel Council. Both student organizations have ranch houses across the street from the campus. Both have memberships that champion radical causes even as they preach peaceful means. Clergyman Lasswell, a red-bearded, heavy-bellied social philosopher, uses sweet reason and street language to keep friends on all sides of all the controversies.

We meet in the Christian Movement headquarters while a group of white students are preparing to turn themselves in at the Van Nuys courthouse for participating in the sit-in. The

33

minister has been helping to raise bail money. He's also been acting as go-between with the police, contacting the accused kids. And now he is arranging car pools so that the accused can commute to jail.

A sign in the Christian Movement living room: "Due to a shortage of trained trumpeters, the end of the world has been postponed three days."

One boy briefs the potential prisoners: "You'll walk in and they'll take your names and they'll photograph you."

Nobody seems upset. A boy and girl play quiet folk guitar. Another boy is drowsing on the couch. The boy doing the briefing says: "They won't book you today. Bail will be set at $250 and the judge will set a later date. Any questions?"

"Yes," answers a young man lifting himself off the floor and raising his hand. "Can I go to the bathroom now?"

At a campus of 18,000 students, the kids in the religious clubs are a minority, the 600 people at a BSU rally are a minority and the 2,000 names on Labovitz's petition are also a minority.

"This student body," smiles psychologist Louis Nidorf, "doesn't really know what it is yet." Nidorf tries to be the academic equivalent of ecclesiastic Lasswell. Faculty member Nidorf serves as a course innovator, draft counselor, activists' adviser and professorial gadfly. Last year he won a distinguished teaching award but he made little progress trying to change the school's general education requirement, a curriculum he calls "terrible."

Wearing an old gray sweatshirt and the beginnings of a grayish beard, Dr. Nidorf says the administration welcomes change but the faculty is frightened. He claims professors still don't know how to make adults out of children:

"You expect someone who graduates from college could go out and become a citizen. But what kind of training has he really had? He's been lectured to—trained to be little more than a comic adolescent."

Five students sit on the grass between classroom buildings looking at a series of nude photographs. As I walk by, a full-bearded boy says, "The trouble is, they came out pornographic." I slow my pace but I can't see the complete pictures.

"Well, I think they're beautiful," answers a girl.

"There have to be two people in them to be pornographic," say another boy.

34

Dan Reagan is a veteran of two previous California colleges and a veteran of Vietnam, where he says he was "healthily scared." At 23, he's a political activist who sits in with the radicals when the situation moves him. Reagan explains, "Right now, I have no absolute commitment, no tight ties to anything. My attitude is if somebody calls me, needs me, then I'll go there."

Shelly Spiegel is a scrubbed-face, braided-hair pretty girl majoring in physical education whose activism has been concentrated in off-campus tutorial projects. She dislikes the Establishment but she has doubts about which movement to support: "I just can't see creating a revolution to put in some people who will do the same oppressive thing."

Senior Alex Clorman shares some of those suspicions: "I'm very cynical and I'm very practical. The one thing a government can't take away is your head or the knowledge you have in it. I want to help humanity—but that's an abstraction. I can only help another individual by helping myself. The way some of the radicals are behaving, we could go through a revolution and remain as ignorant as we were before."

Outside the Counseling Center, an English major admits: "Look, if there were no draft at least 10 percent of us wouldn't even be here. We'd drop out of school and not give a damn—about educational reform or social revolution or spiritual anything. I don't want you to use my name—I just want you to know people like me exist. A lot of us. Probably just as many of us as the kids who are here to get the degree so they can have a payday. If we're usually silent, it's because what we think isn't supposed to be nice."

The Students for a Democratic Society is as troubled as the Establishment about how to locate and shape a majority. At Valley State, the SDS is a changing assortment of individuals, ranging in commitment from nonviolent neo-Ghandism to gun-toting Maoism. Meetings happen in a classroom, more or less on schedule.

SDS is supposed to convene in Room 113 of Sierra Hall at 2 p.m. But at 2 p.m. a regular class is in session.

A couple of SDS members straggle up the corridor, peek into the room and realize that those people sitting there are not their radical allies. One member complains that this always happens. Another is sent up the elevator to scout for vacancies while the rest wait below. The scout returns to announce that there's an empty space one flight above. A girl posts a sign to redirect latecomers. Members come to meetings 15 minutes late—14 students, nine boys and five girls. They shove the chairs into a circle and it looks like any other seminar—no homelier, no hairier than Valley State standard. But, before attacking the agenda, there is one more confusion to resolve. Me.

One of the boys suggests that the press is an unfair manipulator of men's minds. A girl worries that any outsider may inhibit free debate. And Ira Standig, who appears to be leading this session because he is sitting on the desk in front of the circle, says that SDS must make its decision on the basis of what is good for SDS.

A couple of students side with my staying. They plead free speech and individual rights—even if they don't respect newspapermen. Avrum Fried, the minister of defense, also argues for letting me attend. He says that I seem harmless.

Discussion closes. A vote is taken. And by the democratic process, with some 10 affirmative hands, I'm allowed to stay. The opposition abstains.

The new business is almost all educational. Members argue how SDS can best teach the uninvolved and uncommitted. Charging into a building behind the BSU is not enough. One boy worries that black demands are essentially reformist anyway; what SDS has to do is take those demands and make them relevant within a revolutionary context.

Mike Lee, another member, suggests that SDS sponsor classes in the local Experimental College. Somebody else wants to start research on the business-military ties among the state colleges' boards of trustees. And somebody else wonders whether SDS shouldn't initiate workshops in the methods of social change.

Finally, leader Ira Standig says the time is ripe to convert the majority from acceptance to activism. Before the BSU incident, hardly anybody was involved on campus. He says SDS's job now is to enlarge its appeal and build a political power base through education.

I'm sitting there thinking that volunteer classes are about as incendiary a method as the PTA might choose to energize a community. Avrum Fried is obviously making similar comparisons,

36

because he interrupts: "You know, a workshop in East African orgy techniques would draw even more people."

Nobody seconds that motion. The meeting ends without specific plans for implementing the suggestions. My first official exposure to SDS reminds me of my own world—full of the same tangential discussions, circuitous arguments, irrelevant bits of humor. Maybe my presence did inhibit them. I don't know.

Now the members debate whether to rearrange the chairs, from the seminar circle back to the standard classroom rows.

One militant boy wants to leave the chairs where they are. He says it will be a symbolic disruption of the system. Another says nobody will understand the symbolism; SDS wasn't signed up for this room in the first place.

A girl argues in favor of putting the room back in order again. The janitors will be the only ones to suffer if SDS doesn't and the janitors are pretty decent. Why should revolutionaries make work for the workers?

This time, without a formal vote, the SDS straightens up the room.

But Ira Standig has the last words. He picks up a piece of chalk and writes "FUCK IMPERIALISM—SDS," on the blackboard.

This college in the middle of the valley of the middle class is suddenly in the midst of the ferment everywhere.

I used to tell people I belonged to the silent majority," says a girl who still wears braces on her teeth to make them conform. "But now, even if you just want to study without being bugged, you can't be silent. You have to assert that right. And who knows where the majority really is?"

Nobody, for sure. The majority has not formed yet. It wheels with the wind, like Valley's moving sculpture.

POMONA: Exploring Generation Gap

I came to Pomona College full of false confidence, thinking that I already understood students, and that students understood me as a benign middleman who could carry all the important messages between chronological worlds. After all, this was my third campus and I think I'm a fast learner.

Bill Keller corrected me. He's a senior, a campus newspaper editor and a square-jawed clean-cutter—the kind of young man most parents wish all college kids looked like.

We were sitting in front of Pomona's Oldenborg Center and we were agreeing that social pressures at school today are from the left, making liberals out of moderates and radicals out of liberals. Abruptly, Keller stared at my chin and he said, "You must feel like a phony a lot of the time."

"Why?" I asked.

"Your beard," he answered. "Kids do put a lot of stock in buttons and costumes and hair. But you're gonna have to make a helluva lot deeper commitment than that to prove you like us."

In just a few seconds, Keller had destroyed my cover. Indeed, I grew the beard for this campus tour. I thought a modest growth below my mouth would help me look less like a reporter and more like a perpetual graduate student. It would be a badge I'd wear to greet the other generation. Much later, I learned that police and narcotics officers often make the same mistake, thinking they can hide that easily.

"And how are you going to handle dirty language?" added Keller. "Euphemisms, I bet."

"Only for West Magazine and only in rare cases," said I. "All but the bluntest four-letter words will be printed."

"That will compromise your ability to translate students," claimed Keller. "If you can't use students' terms, then you can't express their sense of freedom. If you have to leave out certain words, you'll leave out a certain amount of truth."

He was right again. And adults should know it. From mammoth Berkeley, where the Free Speech Movement began, to little Pomona, college kids use all the words found in public washrooms or army barracks. And students use the words when they're with girls, and when they're at rallies, and when they're with faculty members they like.

The massive stone gates at College Way have a message for all incoming Pomona traffic: "Let only the eager, thoughtful and reverent enter here." Many of Pomona's 1,250 students would like to chisel out "reverent" and replace it with their word, "relevant," as a sign of how they think an 82-year-old private liberal arts school should grow up in the late 20th century.

Pomona is the grandfather of the Claremont Colleges, six separately administered schools which share some common facilities —such as library, theater, church and several academic courses. The campuses are contiguous to each other and to the town of Claremont, where both an art colony and a retirement community live in reasonable peace some 50 miles east of Los Angeles.

Claremont, the town, has neat white frame houses and nicely gnarled trees, still trying to resist the sprawl of steel and stucco from Los Angeles, which already exports its smog through Pomona Valley.

Pomona, the college, is a mixture of modern and Moorish architecture, mostly gray and mainly distinguished by the lawns and malls that become formal gardens between buildings.

This is where nicely turned parents have traditionally sent neat white students. Scholastically sound. Socially correct. A Pomona degree was and is a proper calling card to the upper middle class. Yet I wonder how many parents would have approved of their kid's behavior the October day I arrived on campus, a few hours before the first major demonstration of the season.

I didn't know there was going to be a demonstration. I went to Oldenborg cafeteria at lunchtime to hear a man recruit students for summer work in Crossroads Africa, a Peace Corps-like program. Julie Swan, a lithe English major with ash blond hair and porcelain skin, was escorting me through the food service maze when I noticed the two flavors of ice cream being served. One was labeled banana nut and the other "Abolish ROTC."

A tall, full-bearded student uniformed as a busboy was standing behind the counter, half smiling and wondering whether I would buy a portion of "abolish ROTC," which was mint green. I didn't opt for ice cream but I asked Julie what the sign meant.

She said that the Student Committee for Social Change, an umbrella organization embracing liberals and radicals, was going to march on the ROTC drill field that afternoon. Apparently the cafeteria worker was trying to remind his customers.

Julie had a paper to write, but her boyfriend, zoology major David Hatoff, was going to march. She said he would be happy to take me along.

This is a dreary afternoon for a demonstration. There are sporadic chill showers and the sky is the color of Pomona's grayest buildings.

David Hatoff is worried about weather holding down attendance as we walk a couple of blocks across campus to Alumni Field, which will be the staging area for the march. David is a tall, trim, blond young man who wants to be a doctor. He serves on a student judicial committee and, for fun, broadcasts Pomona football games over FM radio. "I didn't used to be an activist," he says. "I got poked off the fence by what happened last summer in Chicago. Even so, I'm a law-abiding citizen who carries around his little card from the draft board and if the time comes, I suppose I'll go."

About 200 students are already at the field when we arrive, including several with white armbands who will serve as monitors and as intermediaries with campus police in case of any trouble. One SDS member wears a red beret. And one other young man walks about under a hard hat. Several kids wear buttons reading, "ROTC—Rape Of The Colleges."

Bob Berke, handsome, short-haired leader of SCSC—the Student Committee for Social Change—mounts a platform in the center of the athletic field and reads a paper to explain what the protest is about. "Dissatisfaction centers around the apparent conflict between the purposes of ROTC and the purposes of a liberal arts college: the granting of academic credit to ROTC, giving professors of military instruction full votes in faculty meetings

The comforts and clutter of a Pomona residence hall

Mao lines in a window of Oldenborg Hall

and granting ROTC the use of college facilities . . ." These careful phrases are a kind of a compromise.

SDS wants to abolish ROTC altogether, but the umbrella SCSC will be satisfied if ROTC is reduced to another noncredit, extra-curricular activity.

Student body president Rick Marcus, wearing an Air Force jacket over a turtleneck, joins Berke on the platform. Marcus is the new-model militant student politician. He has sideburns that swoop around his ears and they would meet in the middle of his face if his mouth weren't there. He congratulates the protestors and complains that the ROTC has just built a fence around its drill field on the Claremont Men's College campus, obviously to keep dissidents off the grass. Then he warns the protestors that if they force their way onto the field the administration will consider it "obstruction" (and immediate grounds for suspension).

The third speaker is Jim Miller, Pomona's own undergraduate anarchist. David Hatoff whispers that most people consider Miller an uncompromising anarchist because he usually walks around by himself waving his black anarchy flag. He won't join groups or organize them. His participation today is significant.

"We students of these Claremont Colleges," says Miller, looking a little like John Lennon in his droop mustache, "have no substantive power in these colleges . . . America will only be free when the imperialist war machine has been dismantled."

"Some jump," I whisper to Hatoff. "Miller leaps from student power to dumping the Defense Department. Just like that."

"Most of us are still kids," says Hatoff. "Last night, on the eve of this major protest, we had a tremendous water fight in the dorm. There's still an inch-and-a-half of water in the hall. At least Miller doesn't play those games. But this could be trouble today if the ROTC has locked the field and a few guys try to bust in."

By the time Miller is finished there are nearly 400 people ready to march, including a handful of faculty members and even one sympathetic administrator, Dean of Men Roger Bell. Everybody forms a rag-tag double file and I follow along up Mills Avenue toward the confrontation.

As we approach, I count some 150 ROTC students in the midst of drill instruction. Most of them are in uniforms and red helmets; new recruits are still wearing street clothes.

43

The first surprise is the gate to the field. It's open. And there's a "visitors welcome" sign hanging on the fence.

A couple of cadets stand in front of the gate passing out handbills as the marchers go through. The handbills read: "Confident in the knowledge that we can all profit from an exchange of ideas, we welcome this opportunity to talk to you, as individuals, about the ROTC program. We desire dialogue—not disruption."

The dissidents walk in, switch to single file and occupy the periphery of the drill field, gradually encircling the outnumbered cadets in the center. Tactically, the situation is right out of "Wagon Train," with the demonstrators as Indians and the cadets as stagecoaches.

Now comes the second surprise. The ROTC students break ranks. Each cadet picks out a different section of the field and starts talking to the protestors. Suddenly, the area is full of little, separate clots of people.

In one clot, a black cadet suggests that college-trained reserve officers are necessary to prevent a professional military clique, to protect the welfare of drafted soldiers. In another group, a Nisei cadet admits that he needs the ROTC subsidy in order to finish school and feed his wife. A third ROTC student explains that weapon training is no longer offered for academic credit.

The protestors argue in turn, but I'm amazed how amiable they are. And as the dialogues continue, I realize this has become a student-to-student matter, with the ROTC faculty wisely retreating to the sidelines.

After 30 minutes of polite exchange, the march leaders move to the center of the field and rally their forces. Student President Rick Marcus says they should sing the *Star Spangled Banner* with the cadets. SCSC chairman Bob Berke says he wants to sing something else first. Somebody shouts for *We Shall Overcome.*

The National Anthem wins. Some of the dissidents smirk but they also sing. *We Shall Overcome* comes next, led by Marcus and a black faculty member who marched with the protestors. Some cadets drift off the field.

The last selection is the old spiritual *Down by the Riverside.* More cadets drop out. But a few of them stay there, singing in chorus, as dissidents swing into the classic refrain, "Ain't gonna study war no more. I ain't gonna study war no more."

On the way back to the Pomona campus, I tell David Hatoff that this has been the most congenial protest I've yet seen. The

44

military seemed to handle students more gracefully and peacefully than most college administrators. "Yeah, and when you figure 400 students is 10 percent of the six-college enrollment, we had a fine crowd," says Hatoff. "But I really feel disowned by the faculty; so few of them showed up."

We catch up to Jim Miller who is complaining, "Like dialogue is an okay thing, but to have it structured that way by the people you're opposing—wow. The best thing would have been if there were a lot of cops around, then we would have had an enemy to confront."

The Social Action Seminar is a new course, stimulated by students. Each participant is in the midst of an action project in addition to his schoolwork, ranging from tutorial programs off campus to educational change inside the college. The dozen members meet once a week at night in the basement of the Carnegie Building to exchange progress reports with sociologist Noel Chrisman.

This week most of the members were at the ROTC demonstration and they decide to compare notes.

One radical boy says that you can't work up much hostility when the other side takes the role of passive resistance. Another claims to have enjoyed the day, although he wonders whether such dialogue doesn't just postpone the decision about a privileged military cadre on campus. A girl suggests that Jim Miller is really Linus, with a comfort flag instead of a blanket.

And a black girl sums up class reaction: "I came away thinking it was one of those rare victories for reason—absolutely beautiful."

The conversation changes, from Pomona's military life to its social life. "This place," says one girl, "is still not large enough to be a real cross-section and it's small enough so that everybody is always sticking their noses in your business—not as friends—but just to be nosy."

"You start eating by yourself after a while," says another girl, "just so you can have some peace and quiet. Then people start asking, 'Why is she sitting alone?' You can't even enjoy privacy because you know it's bothering them. It almost becomes a neurosis and I used to have my monthly identity crisis. People really doing something outside don't have those crises."

Roughly 90 percent of the Pomona students live inside, at the

45

school. Paradoxically, that makes the campus appear almost empty except when classes are switching. With rooms of their own—in residence halls that now mix men and women—few people loaf or loiter on the grounds.

Even the student hamburger joint, called the Coop, is usually half empty. One afternoon, the most exciting exchange at the Coop is on the front lawn where a young man has an animated coversation with a dog named Ethel. I stand there listening. They pay no attention to me.

Another afternoon, six boys are playing a version of Frisbee football on the Coop grass in bare feet. When the discus-like Frisbee lands on the Coop roof by accident, players argue about who'll do the retrieving. Finally, one boy finds a ladder and climbs it to the roof. As soon as he throws the Frisbee down, his friends pull the ladder away, leaving him stranded.

"Sorry, Spence, old buddy," shouts one of the boys on the ground, "We gotta go to class."

Parents would recognize the Frisbee incident. But would they understand the well-barbered Pomona senior who is having coffee and watching the rooftop foolishness? He's explaining that he doesn't hate his background or his folks—he just doesn't want to have anything to do with either one.

"I don't tell my parents what I think or how I live," he says. "Maybe I'm afraid of what would happen—to them—if they found out what I really was like. I don't know, maybe I just don't want to shatter their illusions. Or maybe deep down I'm afraid they don't have those illusions and they really do know me. And I don't want to know they really know me.

"I think they assume, all parents assume, that a kid has a sense of direction or wants to have one. They think you're more sure of what you'd like to do than you are. For instance, my folks assume I'll find a place in society to fill and that I'll be content with it. They figure my discontent is a phase. Well maybe discontent is a phase. But I'm not about to say it is to them. Because I don't like long hair, they already assume I'm not as uptight as my peer group. They're wrong."

Advertisement on the bulletin board of Walker Hall, a men's and women's dormitory: "Beard and mustache trims, 75 cents. Haircuts too."

Of all the attempts on all the campuses to make life style a respectable academic discipline, the Experimental Residence Project at Pomona is one of the most ambitious and probably the least tethered by administrative strings.

The students call it ERP and burp the acronym, which is a sound of affection covering a yearlong course, for credit, available to 12 young men and 12 young women, sophomores and above, who are interested in the making of a community.

Students were picked on an interdisciplinary basis, so that the two dozen people are a kind of Noah's ark of scholarship, each able to contribute a particular skill to the others. The pioneer ERP group, for instance, includes undergraduate scientists, philosophers, designers, sociologists, historians, engineers.

Dean of Men Roger Bell, the same young administrator who attended the ROTC protest, argued for ERP as a positive way to let students act upon the very questions that haunt their conversations—identity and freedom and aggression and understanding. Bell believes that the time is ripe for new social structures, that modern technology may have made possible "a quantum leap in solving problems of hunger, race and peace." Just as mutual self-destruction may be nearer than it has ever been, so may utopia.

The kids of ERP have a self-contained wing of a dormitory, a reading list that runs from Thomas More to Michael Harrington, and a mandate to make their own experience a legitimate course of study.

They started with no rules. By the time I came to visit, they were already making some rules, having decided that boys and girls sharing bathrooms can be as awkward and inconvenient as the old dormitory visiting hours. But such self-discoveries have not made them conformists.

Sign on an ERP door: "Due to a lack of interest, tomorrow has been cancelled."

One ERP student says he spent last night freaking out on the pleasure of being alive; at 3 a.m. he was touching his fingers and being "naturally stoned while universal truths kept coming into my mind."

A circle of eight ERP students sit on the lawn in front of Clark Hall to talk over their relationships to college and to their families. A bright sophomore named Laurie Johnson with equally bright red hair says, "I came to college because it was the next place. Also for very selfish reasons—to improve myself, to be a better person. As far as classes go, what I've learned may or may not benefit my own life."

Hardly any student mentions going out to make a living anymore; they talk about making a life. I ask the whole group whether they think parents understand the change in emphasis.

"They don't," answers a boy sucking on a blade of grass. "They can't. They read their *Life* magazines and their *Look* magazines and they get these general impressions. Either the magazine perpetuates the beautiful ideal of what the 1950 student was like or it pushes the idea that everyone is walking around with a black flag like Jim Miller."

Then shouldn't a student set the misconceptions straight?

"I don't know," answers one of the girls. "This comes up a lot in discussions about drugs and stuff. Kids keep saying they would never tall their parents. Or they say their parents would never suspect. But then I think about myself. And maybe I'm freaky but I have really good communication. Like my mother asked me point blank near the end of the summer if I smoked dope. In a particular situation, she asked if I'd gone out and smoked dope. And I said yes. She about dropped her teeth."

The circle smiles encouragement and so the girl expands the scene. "She was completely floored and for a few minutes all my mother could say was, 'Oh, my God. Oh my God.' But then later we talked about it and she said, 'Well, you know, my biggest objection is that it's against the law. I wouldn't want you to get caught. And then I think it may have harmful effects.' So I told her I'm really careful and I know the problems as well as she does, maybe better."

Ken Bernstein, the bushy-moustached undergraduate philosopher of ERP, says, "Parents' disapproval isn't the issue. It's whether they find any of this comprehensible. I might reveal some things that might be surprising. Maybe. And they might not find those things comprehensible, almost Jekyll and Hyde. They couldn't see how, with my personality, I ever did that. But I don't think they would disapprove after I'd discussed it with them for a while."

"Yeah," says Laurie Johnson. "Well, I think most parents would really be shocked and horrified if they knew most of the things that their kids did. You know, they may realize in an abstract way, but they can't see their kids doing something and still being *their* kids, *their* children."

Then aren't explanations in order, I suggest, to start filling the generation gap?

"I don't think you'll ever end the generation gap," answers Bernstein. "I'm convinced that I'll be shocked in my own time. If I had a son, say, who was 20 and I was 50 and I found out some of things he was doing, the same things we do now, I'd be shocked. I already discovered I'm like shocked if I see a kid of 13 smoking a cigarette. That's another generation gap. But you know, I also appreciate things like a letter I got from my mother this afternoon after I wrote and told my folks how much I grooved on them, while I apologized if it's sometimes difficult to communicate. And she said, 'I'm not perfect. I never expected you to be.' "

A boy picks his toenail and points his bare foot at Bernstein, "Yeah, but a helluva lot of parents say, 'If you're doing something, then I don't want to know about it.' I've seen those people."

"Or kids *say* that's what their parents say," interrupts Ann Kanter, a girl with a man-melting smile and a maple syrup voice.

"Well, you know most parents haven't really been interested enough in their kids to talk to them," claims the barefoot boy. "If they do talk, then it's about very superficial things that don't make any difference to the kid. They never get on to the level of, 'What are you feeling?' The kid goes along without any kind of honest relationship and then he does something and all of a sudden the parents say, 'How could you do that? Tell us all about it.' All of a sudden you're supposed to confess everything. And you don't even know them, you don't even know them."

Then, I ask, who's doing the protecting? Parents who try to shield kids? Or kids who decide to protect parents from truth? What kind of openness is their generation really talking about?

"You have a point," allows Steve Ringle, a student of architecture who frames his face in steel-rimmed glasses and sings ballads on the side. "But then, who's doing the alienating?"

"Yeah," says one of the girls. "The trouble is some families may even talk to each other but they never touch each other."

The Experimental Residence Project wants to touch. And so the students invite clinical psychologist Jean Kugler to lead them through a session in body awareness.

49

The two dozen experimenters meet after dinner in their private conference room, a sparsely furnished rectangular space on the top floor of Clark Hall. Only three adults are present: counselor Jean Kugler, who looks to be less than 40 years old and more than normally attractive; Dean of Men Roger Bell, who started the whole experiment; and me. The students say I'm welcome to be there but they say I have to participate if I really want to "understand." Okay, I say, having no idea how body awareness works.

Jean Kugler takes over and tells us to take off our shoes and socks and sit on the floor. Then she turns the lights out. The first exercises are simple. In an almost maternal tone, Jean Kugler has us breathe deeply, massage our feet and slap our thighs. I am glad the lights are out because I don't mind massaging my feet but I don't want to be seen doing it.

Now that we have begun to experience ourselves, Jean Kugler puts a Segovia record on the phonograph and orders us up. We have to find partners. But no talking—and so, in the dark, one has to find a partner by touching him or her.

I am fortunate to find a her, a lovely girl with a small nose, bony cheeks, firm lips, long eyelashes and a small pimple on her right cheek. We walk around the room hand-in-hand for a little while, occasionally bumping and touching other couples.

I'm almost relaxed with my new friend when Jean Kugler interrupts the stroll and tells us to do something in a group. We grope around and find six others.

What do you do with eight people who are not allowed to talk to each other? Infantile things. We play a form of silent London Bridges. When we all fall down, the experience is sort of sensual—and then suffocating.

On command, as if this were a square dance, we have to switch partners during the next series. I'm suddenly aware that my body is perspiring and that my bald head is easy to identify, bathing in its own juices. But I'm accepted by the ERP, even in the last exercise when my partner and I take turns practicing artificial respiration on each other.

The lights come back on and a couple of girls come over and say they enjoyed holding hands with me. I thank them formally, never confessing that I'm 38 and really in love with all of them.

The regular ERP seminar follows, and the discussion seems

superfluous after all that touching. The student consensus is that none of the old utopian notions really apply to this time. ERP will have to find its own way, using some ideas from the past; discarding most of the others. Relevant, to them, means right now.

And then a boy in a torn sweatshirt and frayed jeans suggests that time and years are the whole point; Even if ERP figured out an ideal for itself, that ideal would only work for ERP and not ERP's children. "No matter what we do," he says, "we are not going to solve the problem for the next generation."

Right. Little Pomona College is one school where a few bright administrators understand that students don't know their rightful place. And where a few bright students are learning that joy is not necessarily in any place, but in the looking.

That's pretty existential. It's also encouraging, once a parent starts to think about it.

SAN DIEGO:
Signs of Today

I walked onto the UC San Diego campus and immediately saw larger-than-life faces of folk celebrities staring down at me: Bob Dylan, W. C. Fields, Che Guevara, Sophia Loren. They were pasted on high-rise dormitory windows, sharing glass space with other posters, bumper strips, cutouts, collages and tempera paintings

A nude in shocking pink was painted into a window as if she were sitting on its sill. A political message read: "Citizens for Boysenberry Jam." Another window said: "God bless the pill." An eloquent sign language flourishes all over the University of California, San Diego branch. It flashes from bulletin boards and kiosks. It shrieks between buildings.

The sign language permits Argo Hall for men to communicate with Blake Hall for women—facing windows of two large dormitories dressed in social comment instead of curtains.

I walked through the Argo-Blake message center onto the main campus plaza, an open space the size of a city block surrounded by massive modern architecture. There was a solid geometry of buildings to the north and east; a big library-humanities structure to the south, complete with ramps and concrete-lined moat; residence halls to the west. It was powerful and formal and, at mid-morning, almost completely empty. I felt like the only character in a modern version of *Last Year at Marienbad*—dwarfed by pattern and perspective.

I could hear high fidelity rock blaring from several dormitory rooms at a time; it was louder-than-life background music for the outsized faces in the windows. At six-story Argo, the Rolling Stones played against the Jimi Hendrix Experience who played against the Mothers of Invention. There was one second-story window with Bach behind it, but you had to stand right underneath to hear it.

This campus seemed to live by signals, a giant stage full of audio-visual devices but hardly any live action. Other campuses deal in confrontations.

I sat on a wood bench in the plaza and waited for some activity. And just before noon, people began to appear—some of them hauling card tables and bulletin boards to recruit for various campus organizations. I wandered over to a board labeled TNC and read a cryptic message: "Cadre J will meet Thursday, 7:15 in the Revelle dormitory parking lot—we are merging temporarily with Cadre D."

"What does TNC stand for?" I asked a girl at the TNC table with a textbook in her hands.

She looked up, large blue eyes beneath a sheepdog hairdo. She said, "Tuesday Ninth Committee," and then went back to her book.

"Oh," I said. "And what's that? What are the cadres?"

"I'm sorry, I can't talk," she answered, this time keeping her eyes in her text. "I have a mid-term. Maybe you can come back later when there's someone here."

I walked away thinking UCSD is a remarkable place, where you hardly see people and when you finally do, they say they're not really there.

I found other symbolic signs of campus life by going indoors. I almost stepped on a spaghetti-haired boy at Atlantis, one of six low-rise residence halls behind Argo. He was sprawled on the floor of a student lounge. He was studying while connected to a large headset which was attached to a wire which led through a doorway to a phonograph playing in his room. The plugged-in man.

I apologized. "S'okay," he said. "I can't study if there's quiet."

I didn't see any residents in the De Anza Hall lounge but there were two notices on the blackboard: "Will the individual(s) who has (have) been terrorizing this bulletin board contact Don Betts in Rm. 406 before he contacts you?" Just under that threat, in a different handwriting, came the answer: "Get screwed, Betts. Signed an individual(s)."

I looked up Dana Pippin at Argo Hall. He's a clear-eyed,

clean-chinned freshman from Los Angeles whose parents are friends of mine. Pippin showed me his room, a cubicle hardly larger than a walk-in closet. Three beds crammed the walls, a single decker and a double-decker, with aisle-space in between. The lower bunk had drapes all around it like a pullman berth.

"It's the school work," explained Pippin. "My roommate wants the privacy. I have another friend who's a biology major; he has to stay up all night every two nights just to keep up with the workload. This place is very tough and, as you can see, it's very crowded."

I talked to some more students and heard them agree: UCSD is a place of pressure.

The environment is one pressure. This five-year-old university grows atop 1,000 acres across Torrey Pines Mesa, overlooking the Pacific and the town of La Jolla. The ocean is handy for surfing and sailing but the community—full of rich people and retired people—is sometimes hostile to students in its midst. "This neighborhood," complained one boy wearing surplus military clothing from three different services, "is upper rent, upper class and upper tight."

Before the school came to La Jolla, liberals were a tiny minority, Jews were a rarity and Negroes were servants. Slowly, and not without pain on both sides, that's changing. But students who might prefer to live in town can't afford the rentals, so the residence halls are packed—more by necessity than choice.

The academic program is another pressure. Revelle College, the first of UCSD's undergraduate schools, has a science-oriented curriculum and the administration assumes Revelle students are preparing for graduate work. Muir College, the second campus, is more inclined toward the humanities but insists on year-long sequences in math and the sciences.

UCSD is primarily a male preserve because it is science-strong. Boys outnumber girls by about two to one. This produces yet another pressure, according to a student I met while both of us were studying "rides-wanted" notices on the bulletin board in the cafeteria lobby. I asked him about the social life and he told me about the drug life without first asking my business.

"Not much social life," said the boy whose sharp nose contrasted with his rococo sideburns. "I think we probably have more speed freaks (methedrine users) than most campuses because there's so goddam much work and so few girls. At 2 a.m., you can see

Flute play and conversation in UCSD plaza

The geometry of leisure in San Diego

people flying and freaking out on the plaza, after they've finished studying and don't know what else to do. You teach here?"

"No, I don't teach," I told him. I said I was doing research and wondered whether drugs weren't a poor substitute for girls.

"Sure they are," he continued, walking me through the cafeteria line, "but what you have to understand is that people around here are controlled. Even the freaking is controlled. We use drugs as tools now instead of letting drugs use us. A science school doesn't riot. It studies. For some guys, drugs may be like getting drunk on Friday night. For other guys, drugs are another way to do *our* research. We figure classes are only one place to learn; we're also studying things like life style, religion and revolution—kind of all at once." He stopped his tray. "Hey, if you're gonna get to know this place, you ought to hear Marcuse."

I told him I intended to hear Marcuse. After lunch I crossed the Revelle Commons to notice another window message: "Don't spit in the soup—we've all got to eat."

This is the day Herbert Marcuse's undergraduate class meets. Marcuse is the most controversial philosopher in California, the synthesizer of Freud and Marx whose books have become working manuals for American student revolutionaries. Marcuse has been the target of the San Diego press, the American Legion, the La Jolla rightists and conservative politicians; they all want to have him fired. They all keep applying pressure on the UCSD administration and the Board of Regents.

So when I ask a UCSD information executive where to find this besieged celebrity, he hesitates. Then he reminds me that Marcuse has received death threats.

I know that, I say, but my interest is academic.

The information man says he understands but he's not sure Marcuse will; the press hasn't helped the situation any. The executive calls his secretary who calls Marcuse's secretary who promises to check with the professor himself. Back through the same chain comes the message: yes. But I will have to pick up a special pass at Marcuse's office first. The doors to the lecture hall are monitored.

Marcuses's office is above the campus library, light and airy and staffed by an attractive blond secretary. No place to conduct conspiracies.

57

My pass is a green piece of paper with purple print, hand-lettered in blue. Lettered is my name and the underlined phrase, ONE-TIME ONLY. As I thank the secretary, in walks a slightly-stooped, gray-haired sparrow of a man who starts to pour himself a cup of coffee from an urn in the corner. The secretary smiles at me and nods at him, meaning Dr. Marcuse is among us. When he turns to face her with his coffee, she introduces me.

We shake hands, and he asks if I have any "devices" with me. I have no idea what he means but I open my briefcase so that he can look inside where there are only pads and pencils. He explains that he meant recording equipment. And then, in a soft, paternal voice he apologizes. He is embarrassed for having asked and I am embarrassed too.

His course called "The Present Age" meets in the basement of the Humaniites Building. Indeed, there are graduate student guards at the doors of the 250-seat auditorium and I must flash my ONE-TIME ONLY pass at them to enter.

The room is fan-shaped and full. An American flag stands behind the lectern. The students are predominantly freshmen, mostly clean cutters by the lengths of hair and skirts. Dr. Marcuse comes in a few minutes after the hour and his first remark is a request: "Would you please not smoke in this room. There have been many complaints. So repress. Repress." He rolls his "R's" and the students giggle over repression while the philosopher wipes his glasses. The kids lean forward, expectantly.

Today's lecture is basic Freud, all about man's instinctive need for pleasure versus civilization's restraint and repression of pleasure. Marcuse walks as he talks, constantly taking off his glasses and wiping them. He is cordial enough but hardly rousing as he describes the primal horde and goes on to define ego, id and superego.

From time to time, says Marcuse, the primordial force breaks through the repressions of civilization; sons may band together, as in the primal horde, to revolt against the father. Witness the generation gap.

The pimpled boy next to me snickers. I scowl at him. He looks surprised and turns to his notes. At last I have intimidated a student.

Marcuse continues: man's basic drives are sex and aggression. Both are in constant antagonism. There is no such thing as a self-preservation instinct; the need for pleasure supercedes self-preservation. Then, still using the same mild tone, still wiping his glasses, Marcuse concludes, "Aggression in man must sooner or later destroy him—as we shall see next time."

The guru of the revolution is a gentle, repressed personality, I realize. Certainly less aggressive than his critics.

I walk out of Humanities into the plaza just before noon. The TNC—Tuesday Ninth Committee—table is in its usual place, this time manned by a student in frayed buckskin. I still have to find out what this mysterious outfit with the merging cadres is about, so, once more, I ask what the organization stands for.

Tuesday the 9th, answers the boy, was the date of Martin Luther King's death: "TNC symbolizes the death of nonviolence. We're mostly white, organized in cadres to fight racism."

With violence, I wonder, or with nonviolence?

"Depends who you're talking to," he says. "Like I'm interested in what we accomplish, not necessarily how we do what we have to do. Other people are hung up on the idea that you can only honor King's memory by honoring nonviolent means. And then we have guys who say nonviolence died with the man and only force is gonna work in the future. Hell, we get pretty confused but we're the biggest activist outfit on this campus. About 300 students."

The Personal Circus is UCSD's self-discovery outfit, started by students. In 1968, sophomore Tuck Donnelly went up to the Esalen Institute at Big Sur and came back to Atlantis Hall with his psyche full of encounter goups and body awareness sessions and sensitivity marathons. He wanted to bring awareness techniques to the campus, as a way of showing other students that you find expanded consciousness in yourself and not in drugs.

Meanwhile, Donnelly's friends—Tom Peifer, Jim Miner and Barry Wayne—had decided they were tired of talking politics and wanted to try other ways of understanding their world. "I was in this strong political bag," remembers mustached Jim Miner, sitting with his colleagues and me in an Atlantis lounge. "I wasn't getting anything out of it except tensions. Some brought on by the system, sure. But some tensions were really self-repressions."

"Right," says blond Tom Peifer, who has the smile and the gestures of a cheerleader. "The trouble with overthrowing a political system is that you have to get into the same kind of

59

organizations, meetings, dumb bureaucracy—the same kind of crap you're busy trying to overthrow."

The Personal Circus started informally, unofficially, with occasional encounter groups in dorm lounges. This year, in order to accommodate more applicants and have a regular meeting place, the founders decided to register the Circus with the administration.

That's when the trouble started. The dean of students threw them out. Donnelly figures the dean thought Personal Circus was a fancy name for free love or free pot. Their application didn't do anything to reassure the authorities. Where the form said PURPOSE, Personal Circus leaders wrote, "Happiness in human feelings." Where the form called for ACTIVITIES, they filled in, "Varied."

"We really didn't know how to approach them," says Peifer. "One of our ideas was to get started as a language club—you know, nonverbal communication. But it's almost impossible to describe an awareness group."

"You have to be there," says Miner. "Otherwise you wind up talking about what we hope to avoid. We have a high rate of dropouts here and we have a high rate of drug use. There are people on this campus who drop out or take drugs to keep from having nervous breakdowns. The Circus was the only thing that helped the headache I had all last year."

"We're trying to offer a third alternative," says Barry Wayne. "Dropping out and drugs both come from stress. We figure this is a better way to relax and discover yourself within the pressures of the place."

Having failed once, the Personal Circus petitioned the administration with more than 100 signatures. Members promised not to play therapists and they went to the faculty for support and guidance. Along with the second effort came an implied threat: if the school would not register the Circus, then it would meet anyway, underground, without formal permission. The administration has agreed to send an observer to the next meeting.

"But can they really understand what we're trying to do?" asks one of the members.

"I dunno," answers Tom Peifer. "Look at the trouble we're having at our ages. It's pretty difficult to cure 18 years of mind screw."

"I know," says a boy in a cowboy hat. "Personal Circus replaces

60

what people lose when they forget the religion their parents brought them up with."

"Hey, yeah," says somebody else. "Is Father Donovan still here?"

Father Donovan had to leave. He was the nice-looking man wearing a green velour shirt sitting at the back end of the lounge. He's a campus Catholic priest who is also interested in encounter groups. The kids consider him an ally. The idea of religion, more than the ritual of religion, is appealing to students.

"All we're really doing," says a girl in the crowd, "is trying to find a way to hold on and find meaning. I think that's what the old religions were about—surviving, finding meaning. Most of us have come to realize we're not gonna find it in dope or classes or the Movement. Now maybe the difference is we're trying to create our own faiths—but the ends are the same."

Sign on a plaza bulletin board advertising an open lecture: "The Uniqueness of Jesus Christ. All this and refreshments too."

"The Meaning of Anxiety" is a course that meets on the Muir College campus, inside a quonset hut. Muir grows where Camp Matthews, an old Marine Corps base, used to be.

One dozen students sit in a semi-circle around Dr. Jean Mandler, a psychologist and a coolly attractive woman. The kids have been reading the late Paul Tillich and today they discuss whether Tillich's theories on faith have relevance in student terms. It's like verbal volleyball as the students take turns moving the subject back and forth:

"Tillich's idea of a God beyond God means that we have to take the anxiety of meaninglessness upon ourselves. That is awfully heavy."

"Yeah, if you're gonna start conceiving of the inconceivable, you might as well make it enjoyable."

"But you can't conceive of anything more supreme than God."

"Yes, you can. Yourself."

"Unh-unh. Even if you can't accept the Supreme Being that's been crammed down our throats, you have to accept something beyond man. Otherwise you're negating the whole business of being here."

Dr. Mandler interrupts: "Well, if the basic values come from man, then is there any positive meaning to life?"

A boy with basset-hound eyes answers: "Sure, just to stand up and be able to say my life has no meaning means something. That's any affirmation."

I sit there listening to the students bring a theological discussion right down to the level of their own confusions and I wonder how many parents have any idea these arguments cross their kids' skulls. And I wonder how many adults would want to grapple with themselves the same way.

A boy with huge horn-rim glasses complicates this seminar still further: "I think it was Kierkegaard who claimed dread is the possibility of freedom. Then dread could shove you away from faith toward suicide, when possibility and freedom and non-being kind of all become the same thing."

"The basic anxiety," suggests Dr. Mandler, "may be the awareness of non-being." She goes on to say that Freud thought neurotic people were more creative, while Tillich wrote that neurotic people tend to be narrow and timid.

"Well," says the basset-eyed boy, "it's sort of both. When I feel everything is closing in on me, I'm under a neurotic pressure and I have to write something. But when I'm free and I'm sitting on a mountain, I just feel let it come. In the first case I'll try to create something related to the way I feel. And in the second case I may do some thing really new and beautiful."

"But in order to create something new," says one of the girls, "you have to negate something that's gone before."

"No," answers the boy. "See, I'm up there on that mountain and then I'm the first human being who ever lived and I look at the sun and I say that's the sun and then I respond to it. What am I throwing out?"

"Then if the mountain is so good," asks another girl, "what are you doing in college?"

"It's an assignment," he says.

As this class ends I remember the window of Blake Hall which says, "Being is dying by loving." I suppose this means non-being is dying without loving and then I also remember Marcuse quoting Richard Wagner, "The only real fulfillment of love is death."

"The Sociology of Everyday Life" convenes in a nearby hut and I wander over to see whether students can turn the everyday into the cosmic as quickly as they brought the cosmic down to everyday.

62

But this is an entirely different physical setup: larger classroom, ordered rows of chairs, some 50 students. This is a lecture. And although the subject is interesting enough and the instructor is lucid enough, there are four students sleeping before the class is 20 minutes old.

The lecturer pays no attention to them. He contrasts the middle and lower classes, saying that middle people tend to live interior lives in private settings, whereas poor people tend to take to the streets. For many lower-class kids, their neighborhood is their turf and their private preserve, which often leads to conflict with the police who think of a street as a public setting.

A girl in front of me sleeps with her head cradled in her arms and even as I try to concentrate on the lecture, I'm fascinated to see her back as a flag of four colors: hiked up green sweater, pale skin, pink underpants showing above a hiked down pair of brown slacks. Sleepers are themselves a distraction and I find myself beginning to agree with the students who scream for participation in the learning process.

The instructor winds up with a discussion of private morality versus public morality, marijuana being an example. Many people who smoke pot, says the lecturer, privately believe it to be harmless and pleasurable. But they play safe and smoke secretly because there's still a law against marijuana. So public morality, which is the law, often outlives its usefulness in governing private practice.

The students wake up as soon as the lecture is finished. Silence is a disturbance.

I follow two girls out of the hut, across the old Marine base, over the pedestrian bridge above Gilman Drive, and into the Revelle campus—about 10 minutes walking time. While I eavesdrop, they discuss the chemical properties of pot compared to more dangerous drugs. It's interesting but beyond me. So I leave them in the lobby of the Undergraduate Sciences Building, where there's yet another sign of these college times: "Undergraduates wanted to do dull tasks in psychological experiment—$1.67 per hour."

The campus is quiet and quite beautiful at night. Lights warm the insides of the buildings and darkness softens the hard corners of their exteriors. On the grass next to the plaza, a boy and a girl wrestle, laughing, with each other while a dog barks. A steady stream, almost a processional, of other kids go into the library.

The added attractions for this night include an old horror movie showing at the campus Coffee Hut, a visiting radical speaker from UC Berkeley and a student-faculty discussion meeting.

I choose the student-faculty session in the Science Building and take a seat on the far aisle of a lecture hall. Student activist Mike Brown, an extremely bright boy who hides under a black floppy hat and black flowing beard, has told me that sometimes as few as 15 people show up for these things. Usually almost half of them are faculty; professors, too, are curious about this student generation.

Nearly 50 people appear this time, making it a success, but causing immediate procedural confusion. There are 10 professors in the room and almost every one of them seems to have a suggestion—on framing an agenda, on changing rooms, on breaking up into smaller groups.

A student complains that this is typical faculty decisiveness. Everybody laughs but the older men laugh more nervously.

The consensus is to split into sections of about 10 people, with at least two professors attached to each. I tag along behind a group that decides to shop for an open lounge in Argo. We ride the elevator up the high-rise dormitory and I think back 20 years, when I used to have to wait to be invited to see a professor after regular school hours. Here the teachers are coming to the students, wanting to be wanted.

We find a lounge and most of the people, faculty included, sit on the floor. A student charges that the faculty is the most powerful population at a university and he wants to know why the faculty hasn't used that power to push for change.

If that means power to move to the left, answers a professor, then that's what's happening. "The period of appeasing the Regents," he says, "seems to be at an end."

Then would the faculty strike, asks a student, if the situation here ever become as repressive as, say, San Francisco State?

"I suspect," answers a second professor, "that the more radical faculty members are the younger ones—to be truthful, the ones with less to lose should the choices come to striking, quitting, or continuing. But on the establishment side, I think there's something worth saving here at this campus, and I'd hate to see us

64

ever reach an impasse where this university loses its capacity for open inquiry because either repression or revolution has closed us down."

"Okay," answers a student, "but if the university really is a forum for open inquiry, then it seems that the worthwhile discussions and ideas happen outside the classroom. That's wrong. We want to use what we are learning and apply it to the community and ourselves."

The professors nod. And I realize that even under the pressures here the students are doing exactly that. They are doing their things and influencing our things and dragging all of us along with them.

The students are already changing this world. They talk about it while they do it and at UCSD they even post notices about it.

On the way off the campus I took one last look at the residence hall complex. There was a window I hadn't stared at before. "Sex before finals," it said. Just one more outside experiment before academic judgment day.

USC:
Up from Apathy

It was a fresh new semester in 1968 with a clean bright morning
to match. I decided to park a few blocks north of the campus
and walk to the University of Southern California. Small black
children were walking down Hoover Boulevard, going to school,
holding books and lunch boxes. One little boy said "hi" to me
as I passed him on the sidewalk. I said "hi" back and felt the
morning was as good as it looked.

I turned left at 28th Street, where fraternity-sorority row is
a separate swatch of life style between the walkup apartments
of Hoover and the used-car lots along Figueroa. The Row, so
called by friends and enemies alike, has graceful trees and gracious
old houses and some new buildings that resemble Miami motels.

A middle-aged black woman was sweeping the steps in front
of the formal columns at the Alpha Delta Pi house. Two blond
young men, their neat checked shirts buttoned at the backs of
their necks, came out of the Sigma Alpha Epsilon house and waved
at two blond girls bicycling to classes. Ahead of me, a boy big
enough to play defensive linebacker held hands with a tiny red-
haired girl who walked no taller than his Adam's apple.

Most of the fraternity houses were quiet as I wandered the
length of this enclave, a fraternal Greek-letter island surrounded
by city.

USC is an 89-year-old institution founded in what was once
a fashionable section of an infant city. Almost one tenth of the
total population of Los Angeles—nearly 1,000 people—came to
the cornerstone ceremonies in 1880.

USC is the oldest major private university on the West Coast
and while it was growing, the fashionable neighborhood was
changing and the fashionable families were moving north and
west, away from the central city.

A black ghetto moved in, first from south of the campus and then from all sides. Today, USC and fraternity-sorority row stick out as a patch of prosperity in an urban renewal neighborhood. There have been some ugly incidents between neighbors, including the senseless fatal stabbing of a fraternity member by three black toughs. A few frightened people have suggested putting a fence around the university to protect it from the community. A few farsighted people have suggested that USC use its unique situation to become a mammoth laboratory for social progress.

I turned toward the campus proper and passed Alice's Restaurant, a creaky sandwich stand which has its face painted with a Bob Dylan message: "If you're not busy being born, you're busy dying."

I came through the school gates onto University Avenue and sat down on the grass in front of Founders Hall. The brick buildings, the green lawns and the blue sky framed each other beautifully. USC looked like a movie version of what a university is supposed to look like.

I eavesdropped as students gathered at the entrance to Founders Hall, comparing social notes and complaining about academic trivia. Some of the talk was about the vacation just finished. Some griping, among three tall young men, was about athletic scholarships. A couple of other boys stood there judging the pretty girls passing by, especially the ones dressed in extremely short miniskirts and the two or three who appeared to be dressed without brassieres.

Across the campus roadway, long lines of men were renewing their Selective Service student deferments. But nobody at Founders Hall talked about the war or demonstrations or urban tensions. USC is famous for beautiful girls, fine football teams and good graduate schools. Those were the subjects of the morning.

I went down a few blocks to the center of campus and picked up a *Daily Trojan*. The student newspaper wasn't so serene about the world. Editor Mike Parfit's column described the death of childhood optimism: "It's a desperate life when one is young and alone and one stops to imagine. Men disappear and the props that you leaned on break down. Affection is a memory and love just a dream—a magnification of the past focused on the untranslatable future. The stars are cold and the moon drives away the friendship of darkness."

Parfit as reporter was almost as grim. His front page story

summarized a speech by Bill Mauk, the student body president, on the 10 barriers to obtaining a good education at USC. Mauk presented his obstacle course to a group of freshman and the list of woes included: the rules and regulations of the university; the 12 years of elementary and secondary mis-preparation; the four years of college-level irrelevance; the uninspired and uninspiring professors; the outside pressure from parents and other students; the inside pressure from personal crises; the lack of understanding of the black community.

I climbed up the stairs of the student union to see Mike Parfit, expecting to find a young man in the midst of despair. Instead, I found him in the midst of a hamburger, a wide-smiling student whose cowlick reminded me of a hero in the old Our Gang comedies. He offered me a bite of his hamburger but it oozed with too much catsup to pass around. I asked him what the present mood was among USC students.

"I really dunno," said Parfit. "It's difficult for us to keep in touch because this is a very apathetic campus right now. In the first three days of the semester, we've only had two letters to the *Trojan*. And the vocal feedback is very small. But I think things are changing here and it's a good thing. The students are conservative but not as conservative as their parents. Bill Mauk was elected student president last semester as a straight, smooth-chinned fraternity man. Now he's walking around with whiskers and wire-rim glasses. He thinks that's where it's at. That's okay, but you have to be careful whether you're doing something for a cause or just for the pleasure of doing something physical."

Parfit had to gulp the rest of his burger and leave for a meeting with university president Norman Topping. Campus editors are often invited to see campus presidents these days, even at a school with 11,000 full-time students. As Parfit ran out, he said that Mauk's office was in the same building if I wanted to interview him.

A secretary stopped me in Bill Mauk's outer office. Mr. Mauk, she said, was in a meeting listening to a recording; would I care to wait? I would, I answered and through the partition I could hear his now-famous speech about 10 obstacles to education.

A priest from the campus Religious Center also showed up to see the student president. The secretary told him the same

U.S.C. student president, Bill Mark at campus rally

Spring rally at USC

Tommy Trojan; USC symbol of tradition

thing. The priest couldn't wait, he said, and so he left his calling card in the outer office.

Mauk opened his door about 20 minutes later and invited me in. Six other student officers sat around his desk in a semicircle. The president introduced me to them and to a handsome adult who represented the alumni association. Bill Mauk slumped into his chair and tilted it back like a business executive. His new beard began below his chin and when he moved his head forward the beard looked like a 16th century ruff around his neck, bordering regular features and an animated face.

Mauk explained that the group had been listening to the obstacle speech because some parents and some old grads as far away as Chicago had heard about it and were now pressuring the university to find out what kind of radical nut was leading the student body. The man from the administration was somewhat reassured after listening to the playback. Yes, Mauk had spoken informally, sitting on the edge of the stage with his shoes off to welcome the freshmen. Yes, he had quoted Lenny Bruce during the speech, but it was a clean quote: "Out of a source of constant irritation, an oyster develops a pearl." Yes, Mauk himself promised to be an irritation source. And yes, he did say there were university rules that had to be done away with—but not by violent means.

What he attacked was complacency—within the institution and among students themselves. "The role of the university," said Mauk to his colleagues and adult guests, "is to help you find yourself as a person. I wanted the freshmen to start early so I didn't give them the usual back-patting baloney."

This meeting broke up because Mauk had to go to another meeting. I made an appointment with him for dinner and walked outside, just in time to see All-American O.J. Simpson stroll by the bronze statue of Tommy Trojan while one girl pointed and her friend giggled.

I dropped into Mudd Memorial Hall to audit a beginning philosophy class. The instructor, true to tradition, wrote his name on the blackboard, then wrote his office hours on the blackboard and then began his oral presentation by announcing the name of the required text. "Read this book," he said. "It's all you're going to be responsible for in this course." His final opening remarks concerned an essay examination. The lecture that fol-

71

lowed was equally well-organized and equally impersonal. A teaching machine could do as well.

After class I stopped in front of Mudd Hall to read the inscription carved above the entrance: "The Truth Shall Make You Free." And then I noticed what first looked like a gargoyle over the corner of the roof. No, it was a sculpted human head holding a lamp. "Diogenes?" I asked aloud.

"Yeah," answered a girl coming out of the building in a velvet pants suit. "If an honest man ever shows up around here, the statue drops the lamp on him."

Bill Mauk brings Matt Pasternak along for dinner. Matt is a student body vice-president in charge of programs and he's a lean fellow with haunted eyes and a hungry look. We walk off campus over to Julie's, where faculty and football fans eat.

"It's funny," says Bill. "We don't like SC. A lot of us don't. We've thought abut leaving several times. It's not higher education I object to, it's this school. I'm not complaining about campus politics, because politics are challenging and changing here. But I thought college would be a place were students get together and talk about the serious issues of the day. The only discussions you get around here are dating, drinking, drugs and a little sex."

The majority of USC students are from California; almost one third of the total enrollment is from los Angeles. Mauk, however, is from Pocatello, Idaho, and Matt Pasternak's home is Houston, Texas. Both of them chew away on dinner and agree that they have changed at USC, faster than USC has changed.

"I know," admits Mauk, "that if I had the glasses and the beard and said the things I'm saying now, I wouldn't have been elected. The unfortunate thing is that people can always hang me on that point." He smiles, the smile of the accused. "But I figure 98 percent of the students don't have any opinion unless they're forced to have one. And the really unfortunate thing is that there are students who still don't have anybody to talk to. We want to force them to participate."

"Effectiveness," says Matt Pasternak, as if seconding a motion. "That's my main concern."

"We have to assume the moderate position," continues Bill Mauk, "to be effective. But we find the moderate position is

72

considered radical at the institution we're in. You want to see how archaic this place is, go to watch Presents tonight."

Presents is a verb that has become a noun through the years. It defines the ceremonial night when the sororities show off their new pledge classes along Greek-letter island.

I return to The Row after dinner and cars are slowly cruising a spotlit street. The sorority houses are burned by lights as if they were Figueroa used car lots and they have signs on them bragging about the novitiates: "Need we Say More?" is Delta Gamma's slogan for the evening.

The ritual is in process: new girls stand in virginal white gowns in front of their respective sororities. The older girls, the ones who already belong, stand behind them wearing worldly black gowns.

Fraternity men and college boys walk from house to house inspecting the new recruits. If a boy is impressed, he asks for the pledge's name and phone number. If he is mildly interested, he asks for her name. If he is not aroused, he moves on to the next lineup. Presents is not unlike a cattle show. It is also like a high-class bordello celebration, with the girls trotted out for the approval of potential customers. The active members are, symbolically, the madams and they indeed cluck approvingly as young men make inquiries about the pledges.

Parents and alums stand around in the background, apparently enjoying this traditional exercise in belonging. Fraternities and sororities are dying on most campuses because group identity has lost status. The new morality says no one can be his own man unless he is willing to identify with everybody.

But USC is a private school and the Greek societies persevere as a snug system within a system—some all Christian, some all Jewish, almost all pure white. A nice girl on the sidewalk in a black gown tries to tell me that Presents is a misleading sample of the progress being made along the row. "Our greatest example," she says with an absolutely straight face, "is that we had a Korean girl living here for a year. That used to be unheard of at SC but I can tell you we all gained immensely from it."

Most of us adults have believed that we should enlist our kids in institutions when they were college age and we were middle age. It wasn't that we wanted to get rid of them. Quite the

73

contrary. We wanted what we thought was good for them and what would also give us the freedom to resume our lives and to enjoy the results of our hard-earned affluence.

So we send the kids to college and we pay the bills and we expect to relax. The system is supposed to work for us and serve our children because we have worked for it.

But professors and administrators belong to the same system we do. At about the same middle age, they want their sabbaticals and perquisites and the freedom to pursue scholarly lives in research or writing.

Students may be the reason for colleges but teaching is something a graduate student can do. So the keepers of the institutions also assign our kids to a system and go about their personal business. The men best equipped to man the classrooms begin to leave the classrooms.

Then the system struggles along replacing professors with teaching assistants and parents with fraternities. And we all scream ingratitude when the students rebel.

Watching Presents, with bystanding parents all puffed up over such an anachronistic procedure, convinces me that they haven't really been paying attention. The Row represents a dwindling minority—some 15 percent of the USC students—and it's the most self-enclosed institution of them all.

Don Pine is one of the kids who believes he outgrew the institutions. He came here from Scarsdale, New York, bringing the right clothes and holding standard upper-middle-class values. Now, Pine is sitting with me in the coffee house, and he wears the frayed shirt and frazzled hair of a standard radical.

"Two years ago," says Don Pine, "the admissions officer told me not to worry—there were no Berkeley types around here. I pledged a fraternity because I wanted to be accepted and I wanted to go to the Saturday night dances. But the more I learned, the more impossible that life seemed. Guys would go around saying stupid thinks like, 'Cut your hair if you're a real brother.' Or, 'If you have long hair, you look like a hippie—we can't afford to give the house a name like that.'

"Funny, it's okay on The Row to have a mustache or sideburns or have your hair cut Jay Sebring style. That's cool because you see it in the brokerage houses downtown. Daddies and sons get along here because they've both got the same heads. The thing

74

that's tearing houses apart is that half of the fraternity guys are also pot heads. But grass is something you do in secret; it doesn't show like long hair."

Pine likes to write and he also had a radio show on KUSC, the campus FM station. He talks rapidly and nervously, in the manner of a Mort Sahl monologue: "Hell, I'm a new radical. I supported Nixon in 1960 and then Goldwater in 1964. It took me this long to find out that the essential part of the young revolution is to conserve idealism.

"The older generation hates. So how are you gonna throw up your idealism against something that hates? So what you try to do is make yourself appreciate what a human being—other than one who comes from Scarsdale or Palos Verdes—really is. Do your own thing could turn out to be the most important value of all values."

While I'm loitering at the base of Tommy Trojan, a few students are arguing about courses in the Experimental College and what kind of innovations USC needs. A girl with long brown hair, large eyes and slightly crooked front teeth joins them. "No matter how hard you try to make things happen here," she says to a boy with a black mustache, "nothing does."

The others drift away and she sits on the grass eating a ham salad sandwich. I introduce myself and she tells me her name is Joan Jack. "I'm not involved in anything right now," she says. "I wish I were because I feel like a spring—all scrunched up. But the Greeks figure this place is not their problem—and the radicals, the radicals may be just as bad because if you're not hip in their terms, they don't want to talk to you either. They're both cliquey and I don't want to be. I'm not out of the muck yet as an individual."

Joan Jack has moved in both worlds: "If a longhair takes you out, then you smoke pot and listen to a record and it becomes damn dull. If a fraternity man asks you out, then you dance in a stuffy room for five hours and he can't understand why you might want to leave 30 minutes early.

"I'm tired of dope. It's not where it's at. It's so much better to be alive. Not that I'm down on those people, I'm just tired. And I'm tired of the Greeks; last year I wouldn't go to football games because I didn't want to talk to the fraternity pigs or flip cards for the stunts."

Joan Jack commutes but she wants to work in the community:

"People say 'this is a beautiful school, but look at the neighborhood it's in.' Well I think it's a fantastic neighborhood. Look at what the social scientists can learn around here. Look at what all of us might start to understand. You can't go out in Westwood and help anybody or learn anything about anybody."

The Kennedy Action Corps at USC is a student organization involved in seven community projects, from restoring ghetto buildings to counselling ghetto high school students.

Keith Keener, the KAC chairman, is another young adult who has changed in the USC atmosphere. He went to high school in the San Fernando Valley and delighted his whole family by growing up tall with straight features and almost straight A's. His college grades are still excellent but he's become an activist and that infuriates some conservative relatives:

"They used to think I was a precocious little boy," says Keener, "and now they think I'm an obnoxious punk."

Keener leads a KAC meeting in a classroom. His brown, stringly hair is combed and he wears a tie. The members are a mix of former Bobby Kennedy supporters, former Eugene McCarthy supporters, a few Republicans and some independents.

"This isn't a children's crusade any more," Keener tells the KAC. "We're getting off this campus. We're getting out into the streets. Let's just say this campus is not conducive to our kind of activity."

The Young Americans for Freedom are activists from the right. They represent conservatism at the college level and they have chapters at most major campuses across the United States.

The USC YAF meets at 7:30 p.m. in the Student Activities Center. There are only five people—four boys, one girl—in the large conference room and one of them, Bill Steel Jr., is the state co-chairman who has come to listen and advise. "Potentially," Steel says, "this is one of our most important units in the country. SC's got the name and the stature."

"But the fraternities and sororities," says one of the members, "have never been involved in anything here except petty campus politics."

Steel says that YAF will have to change that through education. The old right and the new left use the same rally cry. "YAF," continues Steel, "is for ideology and activity, in that order, on this campus."

The group goes on to complain about the strength of SDS and its disruptive habits. That's interesting; other activists had told me SDS was down to six members and hardly ever held meetings any more. Maybe SDS would be impressed to know there were five YAF people at one meeting, even if USC's YAF had to elect a freshman to be its chairman.

Bill Steel helps the chapter plan a series of special weeks, including one honoring William F. Buckley, featuring guest speakers and satiric publications. "The one thing the new left can't stand," he says, "is humor." Beyond urbane Bill Buckley, I wonder which humorists he has in mind.

Happy Trope may be the most active USC student of them all, an undergraduate critic who says, "USC often stands for the University of Southern Comfort or the University of Second Choice. The truth is most of our brighter students wanted to go to the Ivy League."

Happy Trope, born Roland, is a senior and the first USC product to win a Marshall Scholarship for study at Oxford. He is a member of a student judiciary group, an adviser in a dormitory and an originator-teacher of a seminar called Community Encounter. Community Encounter is also a USC first—a course in contemporary problems taught by an undergraduate for regular academic credit. Trope is in the middle of the system, busily remaking it.

We meet in his cluttered room at Stonier Hall. Trope is short-haired. He sports a drooping sort of Mandarin beard that partially hides a constantly smiling mouth. He throws some books out of a chair so that I can sit down and he begins to tell me that USC has been good for him: "This school allowed me to develop my own kind of liberalism-leftism if you want at my own pace. I've got a habit of trying to solve problems rather than gripe about them.

"I have a love for this place," continues Happy, "because it's given me so much. But I had to kick hell out of it to do it. I think of SC as a bitch; you have to treat her rough and aggressively. The great frustration—the great dishonesty—is to be invited to help make change and then discover your change is not the one the administration wanted."

He lectures to me as he paces around the room and various freshmen pop in to ask campus directions or housekeeping rules. Trope answers them and immediately picks up where he left off:

77

"Social action or change stops at this university once it hits one of two boundaries. The first is cost—if it's gonna cost anything, the administration is likely to say no. The other is sweat—if it's gonna make anybody sweat, especially the alumni, then the answer is likely to be no.

"Our best students graduate with an education equal to Harvard. But the others don't. The A student in political science goes to law school. The B student goes to teach. The C student goes into politics. I'd like to see our politicians better educated." Happy stops, consciously waiting for me to catch up with my notes.

"The SC student fails to realize," he continues, "that he has to change the system or he has to beat the system because he *is* the system. Otherwise, he'll never be able to function in a changing outside world."

Tough, aggressive, baby-grinning Happy Trope even has a few allies up on The Row. For my benefit, he asks his friend Laurie Lynch to arrange a bull session among four or five fraternity and sorority members.

Happy and I walk up to the Delta Delta Delta house after dinner to meet Laurie Lynch who is a senior. She leads us through an opulently furnished, heavily carpeted foyer to the sorority playroom, a bland space that can convert from sitting room to dance floor. Laurie brings an urn of coffee and three others join us to talk about USC for the next three hours.

A member of Kappa Sigma fraternity admits that people on The Row are children of the establishment and, as such, they tend to find less fault with USC than other students. But the men, he says, don't like the Vietnam war any better than other draft-age students.

One of the girls says she is still close to her parents emotionally but can't accept their politics now that she has worked in the ghetto on tutorial projects.

All of the students agree that middle-class parents like to send their kids to USC for the protection offered by a private, essentially conservative school. And sororities, which still have such formalities as visiting hours, provide an added insulation that gives parents a sense of security.

Just before midnight, when the group is beginning to tire, Happy turns lecturer again and tries to summarize why establishment kids and their establishment school have to readjust to a new reality: "Our generation is the one that will really be dealing with the cry for more political power among ethnic groups that have previously been suppressed—particularly the black and the brown. We're talking about equality for them. But that also means a new equality for us, for those who always had the power.

"I don't think a lot of us are being trained for that world where, say, a lot of blacks are in dominant positions and where all people really have the personal power to grow as individuals. The students now at college are not receiving the kind of education that will prepare them for this real equality. I think it was six years ago that the university said it no longer considered its location a liability. But it hasn't yet fully practiced the idea of community commitment.

"If we go out of here as adults, unprepared for this challenge of equality, then that will be the tragedy of our generation."

The others nod. No arguments.

We leave the Tri-Delt house just before sorority curfew and we have to weave through clots of boys and girls necking on the porch, the lawn, the sidewalk. The neckers are oblivious to us and oblivious to the neighborhood. Their eyes are closed and, for now, they still belong only to each other.

SAN FRANCISCO STATE:
On Strike!
Shut it Down!

There was a declared strike and an undeclared war when I was at San Francisco State College. The longest, bloodiest confrontation in the history of American higher learning began in the fall of 1968 and continued, with sporadic outbursts of violence, into spring of 1969. Then it seemed to be over. But this troubled school will be a long time recuperating from more than 500 arrests, dozens of injuries to students and police, several bomb incidents, a few fires and a partial faculty walkout. Amazingly, no deaths.

Students brought guns to campus at the height of the conflict. Police carried guns on campus. Students used walkie-talkies to communicate with rebel allies. Police wore portable radios to keep in touch with shifting combat positions. Students threw rocks and bottles. Police fought with three-foot clubs.

It was not at all like a sit-in, which has a comprehensible beginning, middle and end—angry dissidents lock themselves in a building until a superior force drags them out. A sit-in has a fixed point of geographic reference, the building. When a sit-in is over, a campus returns to academic business.

San Francisco State suffered a guerrilla action that spread through the entire urban campus, erupting in unpredictable places on unpredictable days. There were no fixed positions. In the early days, police generally held the buildings and regrouped in basements. Students massed on the lawns or staged raids from the campus periphery.

The war had hours, however. Nights were normally peaceful. The rebels usually arrived early in the morning for strike duty.

The incendiary rallies were at lunchtime. And the battles happened in the afternoon. By 5 p.m., the revolutionaries almost always went home to dinner. The cycle would start again the next day during the regular working hours.

San Francisco State is a commuters' school, whether somebody is commuting to classes or combat. Nearly 18,000 students are enrolled there, and less than 10 percent of them live in residence halls. The majority of San Francisco students have paying jobs while working toward a degree. They are older than the average undergraduates at other campuses. They are mainly city people—and some of them are street people, having grown up in lower-middle-class neighborhoods or in the San Francisco ghetto, which is only 10 minutes away.

I drove through the Fillmore ghetto on the way to the college, a cracked-sidewalk commercial neighborhood full of small dry-goods shops, liquor stores and vacant enterprises which have been covered over with political posters.

I began to see the swarm of hitchhikers after I turned onto Market Street and started winding up Twin Peaks toward the campus. The sky was washed blue, the fog had lifted, the whole Bay Area spread out below me and the windows of the buildings were blinking reflections of the sun. I picked up three boys who were carrying books and, as we approached the middle-class community bordering Lake Merced and the campus, I asked them about the strike that had been called by the Black Students Union only a few days earlier.

"I dunno," said the boy in the front seat. "I think there are 10 demands but I'm an engineering major and I don't figure to be affected."

We had to park six blocks away from the school. Kids were arriving by streetcar, motorcycle, car pools and hitched rides. Some people came to S.F. State that morning to attend classes. Some came to picket. Girls handed out flyers to everyone coming through the entrance at Holloway and 19th Avenues. Several white activist groups were helping out in support of the strike.

I collected one handbill that listed the 10 demands of the BSU. I accepted one presenting the administration's position concerning the strike demands. I took another that listed the position of the Third World Liberation Front, extending BSU demands to cover

81

the wants of all ethnic minorities. The paper blizzard had only begun. There were three free newspapers available on campus that morning: *The Daily Gater*, published out of student funds and reflecting the militant position; *The Phoenix*, published by the journalism department and attempting to find a middle ground; and *Strike Daily*, a radical journal fianced by radicals.

I made my way through the rows of people petitioning me with papers, past the Administration Building and came to the campus commons, a large open space surrounded by San Francisco State's homely stucco buildings. It looked like a large high school. A heroic-sized man with a beard that hung above his bare chest was selling the *Berkeley Barb*, an underground newspaper competing with the handbills.

The grass was littered with throwaway periodicals, milk cartons, sandwich wrappers and dirty dishes on abandoned cafeteria trays. Nobody was picking up anything. I suppose it's silly to clean an area if a riot is expected.

The facade of the cafeteria, facing the commons, blared with posters and banners. "STRIKE," said the largest banner above the entrance, "If You're Not Part of the Solution, You're Part of the Problem."

Several bridge tables were set up along the walkway manned by assorted student groups handing out more propagnada. Stray dogs wandered around sniffing at the dirty dishes, occasionally chasing each other. Students sat on facing rows of benches in front of the cafeteria, separated by the walkway and a snaking piece of funky sculpture made out of barbecue ovens strung together with chain. More than 100 kids milled about, apparently not going to their 9 a.m. classes. I sat on one of the benches and the crowd seemed to melt away from me. Plainclothes officers had been assigned to mingle among the students and maybe I looked like one. I walked around behind the benches and heard a white boy apologizing to a black student: "Look, I've tried to get those bastards to honor the strike. They say they support the demands but can't afford to miss the class."

A black adult, in tie, came by and a girl shouted, "Do you support the 10 demands?" "I helped write them," he answered. The man was Dr. Joseph White, S.F. State's 35-year-old dean of undergraduate studies. White, a hip-talking clinical psychologist, turned out to be one of the few agents who could cross the lines and talk to both sides during the months of warfare.

Girls and grafitti of San Francisco State

Conversations among San Francisco commuters

Student amidst the littered lawn of SF State

I introduced myself, and Joe White told me he had been a student at S.F. State in the early 50s and that the place had always been a school for city kids and a school for educational change, close in time and feeling to the community around it. But there used to be prorortionately more black students in the old days, before the California college system became a statewide bureaucracy.

Joe White also helped draft the proposal for a Black Studies program that was the key issue in the strike. Although black-oriented courses were already being taught at S.F. State, they were scattered through several departments, and the school had not fully established or staffed a Black Studies Department that could grant a bachelor's degree.

He said the academic questions were blurred when the strike was called. People on both sides were talking about tactics instead of substance. So Joe White was operating in what he called "the field," going from faculty conference to BSU caucus to administration meeting.

I asked him if the strike was successful. He suggested that I drop into some classrooms and see for myself. And so I began a short course in campus revolution.

This is an anthropology class and a white student has just barged in, waving his arms, interrupting the lecture and urging the 60 students to leave the room in support of the BSU. The teacher invites the intruder to take five minutes and present his case.

The boy tells his all-white audience that S.F. State is a racist institution and that it will remain racist unless white students refuse to attend school until the BSU's non-negotiable demands have been met. Then he walks out.

A few students laugh. Three students leave the room. The teacher takes over and says it may be impossible to conduct classes with such constant harassment. He asks how many students would be willing to meet at night for the next few weeks? About half the students raise their hands. A pimply boy turns to the blonde girl next to him and says, "Well, this is one way to get smaller classes."

On the way out of the building I notice two glass doors boarded over with plywood. They were broken last week by the rebels.

Before lunchtime, on the grass in front of the cafeteria, 10 white boys and girls form a circle and announce they are about to perform a little guerrilla theater for the bystanders. One of the boys pulls a red plastic pig mask over his face and starts beating the others, yelling, "Get to class, get to class." More than 100 students watch and applaud.

A second group leaps onto the grass. These students identify themselves as majors in the drama department, and their presentation for today is a pantomime on police repression called *A Man Looks at the Sky*. It's street theater and it's over-simple but it's effective, because the players are intense. I wonder whether they work as hard on class productions. Maybe the strike, in a perverse way, sharpens their creative energies. I do know that, with all their unhappy side effects, college disruptions are also learning experiences.

As the theatricals end, a girl in the audience runs around saying, "Hey, I'm trying to find somebody in my psych class. I didn't go and I want to know the reading assignment."

The BSU rally begins just before noon on the platform in the commons. I hadn't seen many of S.F. State's 800 black students during the morning. Now several clusters of black boys and girls stand around the grass. "There should be nobody up there in the classes," says BSU spokesman Nesbitt Crutchfield. "Those people are eating and growing fat and vacillating . . . They should be out here."

Crutchfield is militant and homey at the same time, a style that pleases the 200 or more students listening. "We had some plainclothes pigs out here," says Crutchfield, timing his phrases like a veteran politician, "trying to look like righteous students. But you could see the flies around their heads. Flies. You couldn't miss 'em." Crutchfield introduces a white blue grass band that plays *I'd Rather Be a Newsboy in the U.S.A. than a Ruler in Some Foreign Land*. The crowd laughs. Then William Stanton, a white faculty economist, takes over and delivers a rather dull lecture about racism.

Over at the cafeteria, a young black man in a business suit sells the Muslim newspaper and two elderly people sing *Wonderful Is My Redeemer* in front of a sign saying, "Jesus Christ Saves from All Sin." While the evangelists and the Muslims and the BSU are making public appeals, the S.F. State faculty is meeting in the campus auditorium. I walk over to the lobby and discover TV cameras focused on Ben Stewart, the BSU chairman, who explains that his organization cannot accept a faculty negotiating proposal. Even here, as teachers file through on the way to their convocation, the BSU has upstaged attention.

I attempt to sneak into the meeting and can't. A campus policeman demands to see my faculty ID card. So back I go to the commons rally, just in time to watch professor Cyril Roseman take his negotiation ideas directly to the BSU. There are now some 2,000 students in a wide semicircle around the platform.

"C'mon up, chump," says one of the BSU leaders to the chairman of the Urban Studies Department.

Roseman, a young medium-short, wavy-haired man, accepts the invitation and tells the students, "I do not believe this campus at this time is in a position to resolve the struggle of the black people." Black people in the audience heckle and hoot. Roseman says he is in favor of the 10 demands but he does not approve of the strike. "If we want to bring this campus down," says Roseman, and suddenly the audience cheers, "then let's go ahead and do it." The audience roars. "But if," Roseman starts his next sentence. He can't finish it. A BSU leader grabs the mike away from the teacher and tells him he's said enough.

"Let him talk," shouts a student in the audience.

"Let's vote," says a BSU member holding the mike. And then the ayes and no's shout at each other. From where I'm standing in the rear of the semicircle, it sounds like Roseman has won his second wind. But the BSU interprets the loud nays up front as carrying the day. "The people rule," says the BSU man, nudging Roseman off the platform.

A white women in the audience, wearing a crucifix and carrying a book of Milton's poetry, is horrified at the indignity to a faculty member. While the rally drones on, she begins to argue the virtues of nonviolent dissent with a black woman standing near her. The black woman tells her to shut up. The white woman continues to scream for free speech and against force when, suddenly, in the midst of her plea for reason, she slaps her black antagonist. The black woman hits her back.

The white woman, crying, arguing, trembling, is pushed out of the audience by other students.

I return to the faculty meeting in the auditorium at 2 p.m., hoping that maybe the guards have stopped checking identification. I'm in luck. A friendly administrator tells one of the gate-keepers to let me through.

I haven't missed anything. There are 500 teachers in the hall—almost half of the S.F. State faculty—and they've been in session most of the day without resolving any issues. There are two microphones in aisles on opposite sides of the auditorium. Professors are lined up behind the mikes, each waiting a turn to enunciate a personal position.

The only substantive vote of the afternoon is to censure California State Colleges chancellor Glenn Dumke for ordering the suspension of instructor George Murray. Murray, a Black Panther and graduate teaching assistant, had allegedly advised the black students to bring guns to campus for their own protection. Dr. Dumke ordered Murray's suspension before the S.F. State administration investigated the incident. Teachers are furious because they believe Dumke has denied due process and thereby helped precipitate the strike.

The only other resolution that passes is to continue the extraordinary faculty session at 9 a.m. the next morning. Professors talk about acting. Acting, for them, is talk.

The campus begins to empty by 4 p.m. There are three dozen reporters in the Administration Building waiting for the daily press conference, and one of them complains, "This is like sitting in Saigon."

I go up to S. I. Hayakawa's office in the Humanities Building because someone says that the famous general semanticist is preparing a statement on the strike. Hayakawa, a stocky man with owlish glasses, is cordial. But he's upset.

"There are a number of white students," he says, "who identify with Negroes so profoundly they want to be Negroes. But it's not the students who bother me so much as my colleagues who seem to be middle-aged adolescents and have this compulsion to fight Dumke, this absolute need to shake their fist at authority figures."

Hayakawa indeed has been preparing a statement for presentation to the faculty. It begins, "I wish to comment on the intellectually slovenly habit, now popular among whites as well as blacks, of denouncing as 'racists' any who oppose, or have any reservations about supporting the demands or tactics of extremist black organizations." His statement goes on to label BSU disruptions and

88

threats as gangsterism: "There are many whites who do not apply to blacks the same standards of morality and of behavior that they apply to whites." This attitude is itself a form of racism, according to Hayakawa. Later in the S.F. State war, he was to become president of the embattled college.

On my way out of the campus, while I'm walking and writing myself a note about how comparatively peaceful the strike has been so far, somebody whacks my elbow from behind and tries to snatch my papers. I turn and it's a tall skinny blond kid who runs by laughing and says, "Press off campus."

Dawn barely lights the cloud cover, a gray beginning for the day. But the sun bursts through by 8:30 and there are more than 100 people, almost all of them white, on the picket lines. Some 30 faculty members join the strike circle marching around the main campus entrance, the first visible support from teachers. They carry small red signs reading, "Faculty Strike for Campus Autonomy." Only faculty members would use the word "autonomy" on a poster.

The mood is folksy. San Franciscans on their way to work lean out of their cars along 19th Avenue and shout pleasantries or curses at the pickets. The pickets smile. Then the teachers break ranks and start off to the morning faculty meeting. I follow them and today the doorkeepers do not question me.

President Robert Smith opens the session and apologizes because he can't stay. But he's sure, he says, that word of the proceedings will come to him from the academic senate or the news media. Several teachers hiss the media.

Now the paper blizzard moves indoors. Members of almost every faculty department have prepared resolutions for presentation today, and dozens of mimeographed proposals flutter through the rows of the auditorium. The strike, by default, is already effective: these teachers are away from their classes.

Humanities wants to support Smith, prohibit disruption. English wants an immediate Black Studies Department. World Literature wants to try arbitration again. Psychology demands local autonomy. Business wants the faculty to disassociate itself from the students' strike. Philosophy urges the immediate rehiring of Murray.

The proposals conflict, overlap, confuse. For two and a half hours a parade of speakers attempts to frame the proposals in

89

a form suitable for a faculty referendum. I go out to the lobby to stretch and I overhear a black girl telling a friend, "The reason they won't let students into these meetings is they don't want students to know how PhD's deal in irrelevant bullshit. After all, these are their teachers."

Some classes are meeting on the lawn today. Over at the commons platform more than 80 white students are having a forum on what activists should do during the strike. A majority of these kids are supporters of the BSU, but some of them complain about the apartheid on campus—black militants won't talk to them. "That's because they don't trust you," says a bearded boy. "They know you can go back to your middle-class security whenever you want to. That's why they don't trust the SDS. The SDS can crawl back into the shelter of a white skin. The BSU can't turn around. That's the difference."

Only about 100 yards away, on the same center lawn, a boy and girl wrestle. He pins her to the grass. Her blouse hikes up and her belly shows. She laughs and shouts, "Are you gonna rape me?"
He laughs and lowers his face to hers.
"Not here," she screams.

The BSU has a press conference at 12:45 behind the BSU hut, which is one of several wooden shacks housing S.F. State student organizations. All the shacks are clustered near the side entrance of the cafeteria, eyesores on a campus that has neither architectural charm nor a student union to house undergraduate activities.
Two dozen reporters and TV people show up. We are not invited inside the hut; no whites are. About 40 BSU members, many of them wearing the black jackets and black gloves adopted by the Panthers, form a circle around the press. A portrait of Huey Newton holding a rifle is tacked on the wall. It serves as a backdrop for the camera men.
Dean Joseph White opens the conference as the administration's liaison to the BSU and announces that the students will not discuss tactics today. White introduces BSU chairman Ben Stewart, who reads the 10 demands, stressing a fully implemented Black Studies Department and the rehiring of George Murray.

90

Nathan Hare, the sociologist who came from Howard University to head the acting department for the Black Studies program, says that other schools are looking to San Francisco State for leadership. And George Murray appears, flouting his suspension, to claim that this strike marks the first time in the history of the United States that nonwhite ethnic groups have dissolved the barriers between them. "The goal," says Murray, smiling and savoring the words, "is the seizure of power." If the teachers do not support the strike, he continues, then they're "racist dogs, punks, bootlickers."

It is not what you'd call a relaxed press conference. The non-speaking BSU students are a silent circle of hostility. The reporters and cameramen jostle against each other. A TV cameraman from San Francisco makes matters worse. As the conference ends, he tells nearby reporters that he was jumped this morning by a black kid who kicked him in the back and dented his equipment. The BSU and the press are so closely wedged together that a couple of black students start yelling "liar" at the photographer.

I begin to work my way outside the two circles, thinking the cameraman has picked a peculiar place to complain. Just as I reach the side entrance of the cafeteria, I hear white students start screaming, "Here they come!" And so I jump on an outdoor table to see a blue line of nine policemen marching toward the hut area. They are helmeted, armed and carrying yard-long clubs. They are members of the San Francisco Tactical Squad, an elite unit assigned to quell civil uprisings.

The police proceed to an open space in between the BSU hut and the cafeteria, then they stop. Nothing happens for what seems to be a whole minute. The police stare at the BSU and the members of the BSU stare back . . . an incredible tableau of mutual distrust. Then hundreds of white kids surround the police from the rear and shout, "Pigs off campus!" A few white kids begin to throw dirt clods and bottles. The verbal abuse swells to a chant, and then a wail as students turn into a mob. Suddenly the police break ranks and wade into the crowd swinging their wood batons like baseball bats. They hit bottle throwers and they hit innocent bystanders.

The students start running in several directions, screaming, swearing. Somebody knocks me off my table and then I realize that I'm running too, away from the dull thunking sounds of clubs

91

hitting human heads, away from the lunatic kids who are grabbing rocks and heaving them blindly into the battle. I run about 200 feet and then, ashamed of my own panic, I turn around and go back to the huts as the police drag three students—one of them BSU sokesman Nesbitt Crutchfield—across campus toward Holloway Avenue.

There are three police vans waiting at Holloway. The police lock their prisoners in the vans and form a wall between the vehicles and several hundred students who have followed the Tactical Squad. Most of the reporters are standing in the street, including the TV cameraman who complained about being jumped.

As the police start to drive off, a few white students run toward the cameraman. Somehow, the word has been passed that he may have inspired this riot. The photographer runs down the sidewalk. The kids chase. It looks funny for a few seconds, like hare and hounds. Then the photographer stops, tenses and swings his camera at the kid nearest him. The boy falls into a hedge, his head bleeding. The police return immediately and reverse the chase up the street. They beat up another boy and arrest him. The sun is still shining but this has become a horror phantasy as both sides take turns behaving like animals. A girl sits on a low wall crying, "Why can't they leave our campus alone?"

"Do you mean the police or the strikers?"

"Get the fuck away," she answers.

The nightmare recurs the same afternoon. A group of students attack a campus policeman near the Psychology Building. The tactical squad comes to his rescue, and a new crowd of students scream. The cops swing. But this time a line of 40 teachers marches into the fray, interposing themselves between the kids and the tactical squad. This time, the new tactic works. Both sides become human again. And I hear students shouting, "There's Stanton! There's Solomon! There's Miss Boyle!" picking out favorite teachers as if they were cheering at a football game.

At their marathon meeting, the faculty votes to close down the school in the interests of safety.

The radical students reconvene at the commons platform. A boy speaking for the Third World Liberation Front says, "Now nobody goes to school, nobody." The white boy who was hit by the cameraman stands up on the platform, his head still bleeding,

92

and shouts, "press brutality." A BSU speaker says, "The argument about violence is now irrelevant; we're talking about the struggle of the people."

A white girl grabs the mike to plead for nonviolence, crying, "You're all turning into what the cops are." The crowd boos. A white boy offers a battle suggestion: "If you're gonna throw the goddam rocks, then aim them. There were more kids hurt by rocks today than pigs." A few minutes later, the rally crowd surges toward President Smith's office in the Administration building. I look at my watch, astounded: it's only 2:30. I feel like I've been standing or running for 12 hours. Some 500 students clot outside Administration chanting, "We want Murray." A blond boy points a bullhorn in the air like a trumpet and shouts, "That head pig Smith better get out here right now."

A cadre of BSU members push their way through the crowd and walk into the building. The other students immediately stop shouting. The sudden silence is terrible and I stand on the terrace of the Administration Building wondering whether the BSU is going in to talk or to terrorize.

President Smith responds to their arrival. He comes out of his office and stands on the steps to address the students. He is a short man, immediately lost among taller students. Smith tells the crowd that the police are on campus for the safety of the people on campus. He never completes another sentence. Students hoot, curse, shout him down.

At the regular late afternoon press conference, Smith tells some 50 reporters that he has decided to close the campus until it can be opened on "a more rational basis."

I learn that the incident involving the TV cameraman indeed started the violent confrontation. An administrator called the Tac Squad on campus to find out whether the photographer was able to identify his attacker at the BSU hut. The photographer couldn't, which seems to be why the police stood there waiting until the mob incited the riot.

A magnificent piece of stupidity. Whoever sent the cops to confront the BSU at the end of their press conference is the man who helped convert a semi-successful strike into a total shutdown.

By 5 p.m., the campus is quiet again. I walk out to 19th Avenue and pick a handbill off the ground. It's a new one. "Had enough,

Whitey?" it begins, and the message is a one-page piece of pure hate from the American Nazi Party. Everybody has moved into this act.

I pick up a hitchhiker who introduces himself as Pike Oliver and says, "Well I guess I can hang it up for this semester. Pretty damn sad when you realize there's nobody on any side you can go to, talk to, admire."

There are no cheerful pickets this morning. The usually crowded, littered campus is only littered. A few faculty members precede me to the auditorium. I go inside and count 50 teachers already present.

President Smith walks up to the platform. The faculty applauds. Then half the teachers stand to give him an ovation. The others stare straight ahead, withholding support. The president says that he is in no hurry to reopen the school. The general response is relief.

Then the faculty resumes its parliamentary arguments. Even on the day after the horrors, debate becomes so tangled that an English professor rises and says, "I wish to offer a substitute to the substitute motion." This is a refinement of yesterday—when someone offered an amendment to an amendment.

The meeting breaks up before lunch. The faculty now knows that the last few days have only been the beginning. The faculty senses that Smith will soon resign. The faculty realizes that nobody is in control.

I walk out in the almost empty commons and try to figure out what I would do if it were my school. I think I'd start by forming a student-faculty joint force to protect the campus population. City police cannot stand insults and missiles without resorting to their clubs. Militant students cannot stand police presence without resorting to ineffable abuse. Police have become the chief incitement, to be removed as a start toward peace. Joe White was right. The issues are almost forgotten. The tactical war has begun.

I drove to the San Francisco airport and heard, on the car radio, that the governor and some legislators and a few members of the State College Board of Trustees were infuriated by the abrupt closing of San Francisco State. Closing down was an affront to education and to their pride. They were demanding that the school open immediately, using whatever means necessary.

They were wrong. But then they weren't there. If San Francisco State had been immediately reopened, it would not have been a school but a shambles. A shambles is a slaughterhouse where animals are killed. It was approaching a shambles when I left.

STANFORD:
Testing Tomorrow

Final exams are among the few constants of university life. Confrontations erupt and subside. Old rules are thrown away as quickly as old school ties. Courses are in continuous flux. But finals are still the fearsome days of reckoning and Stanford University was in the midst of them when I arrived one downcast, drizzling morning.

The drooping eucalyptus trees near the main entrance shed high tears and low bark. The upright palms lining the mile-long approach to the 80-year-old campus looked like mammoth umbrellas, their tops torn by the rain and waving with the wind. A girl bicycled in front of my car, her red plastic raincoat matching the red roof tiles of Stanford's buildings. Her head was covered by a yellow hat but her long yellow hair streamed out from underneath, tangling across her back like seaweed. I beeped my horn as I went by and she turned to smile, a Lorelei in large-rim glasses.

The students who walked to their exams stayed under the covered arcades that frame the old sandstone classroom buildings. They moved slowly through the arches—the pace of penitents comtemplating their faith at a monastery.

I parked near Jordan Hall, one of the old Romanesque buildings being renovated to accommodate Stanford's 12,000 student bodies. The plywood construction fence surrounding the project was full of graffiti and one particular message summarized the combination of blasphemy and reverence—of risk and tradition—I found all over the Palo Alto campus.

"IF GOD WERE SPELLED BACKWARDS," said the sign, "HE WOULD STILL BE MAN'S BEST FRIEND."

No major university in the country has tried harder than Stanford in the last several years to stare at itself in the mirror, to look at its power backwards from the students' point of view, to anticipate the upset of former ideas. Stanford is the wealthiest, most prestigious private university west of the East Coast; it is also willing to chance change.

Stanford was among the first institutions to encourage truly coeducational residence halls. It was one of the first schools to offer a major in Afro-American studies leading to a bachelor's degree. It pioneered the establishment of overseas campuses and now there are five branches of Stanford scattered through Europe. It is in the midst of a three-year overhaul of its whole institutional philosophy called the Study of Education at Stanford, the project of a faculty-student committee determined to make the school as responsive to undergraduate needs as it is to trustees' decisions.

The place absorbs newness, partly because Leland Stanford's 8,800-acre farm gave the university an extraordinary great green space to grow in, partly because the several new buildings have the same earth-color exteriors as the originals. I wander around in the rain and decide that this is probably a campus that all the old grads will always recognize. They won't like the SDS newspaper—the *Street Wall Journal*—pasted on a temporary fence. And maybe they won't admire the two full-bearded boys coming out of the bookstore, even though beards seem to suit a sprawling educational park where there are more lawns than parking lots.

At Tresidder, the new student union, I walk inside the game rooms to see whether people are playing during finals week. The bowling alleys are absolutely empty. There are four boys shooting pool and one of them complains that he's rushing his shots because of an afternoon language exam.

I find Denis Hayes, the student body president, in his office upstairs at Tresidder. He's a gaunt, ascetic-looking man who, at 24, calls himself the oldest undergraduate on campus. Last year, after probably the most widely-photographed student campaign in the history of the United States, Hayes defeated a topless dancer named Vicky Drake whose candidacy advanced such apolitical measures as 38-22-36. Hayes upon victory said: "Surely there can be no stronger indictment of the sandbox nature of our contemporary student government than the platform of my recent opponent."

The students downstairs in the cafeteria look forlorn, eating sandwiches with one hand and turning texts with the other, so we drive off campus for lunch. History major Hayes is not only older than his constituents, he's also more traveled. He interrupted his education to work his way around the world—Alaska, Russia, Africa, Europe—before coming back to Stanford.

"This is the best institution in the world for me," says Hayes. "To the extent that I could love any institution, I probably love Stanford. Most people's impression here is love at first sight. Then they grow to hate it. And then some learn to love it again. To the extent that love grows out of marriage. I probably love Stanford."

No other student politicians have talked to me that way. Most of them either despise themselves for becoming stooges of the system or they despise the system for its own immobility.

It isn't fashionable to announce a college loyalty but Hayes, who weighs his thoughts before broadcasting them, has outgrown fashion. He is wise enough to know that universities are infinitely complex; they have more intricate cogs and levers and balance wheels than a Rube Goldberg cartoon. His presidency has been an attempt to explain how the boggling machinery works and he tries to bring students into the procedure. Most undergraduates, Hayes says, have no real knowledge of how power is delegated from the trustees to the university president to the faculty. And while his classmates may consider him a middle-of-the-roader, Denis Hayes has been actively pushing for a fairly radical ideal: the resignation of some Stanford trustees to make room for student representation on the board. The school already has students on almost every committee influencing campus life, including a joint student-faculty judicial group that has legal power in disciplinary matters affecting teachers as well as kids. But power is a dangerous exercise unless it is completely understood and so this old man of an undergraduate president is wary of most movements.

He characterizes Stanford's SDS as a collection of students with deep moral concern but little comprehension of when to move, or how to shift the bulk of undergraduate opinion. He admires Stanford's BSU but says the 250 black students on campus are essentially middle class in their life styles, regardless of their rhetoric.

As for the silent majority, Hayes says: "They're silent because they don't have a helluva lot to say." He has been as worried about the conservative students as the radicals. "I'm really afraid,"

Understanding at Stanford

The grafitti of Stanford

he says, "that maybe kids on the right will take matters into their own hands during a radical demonstration to produce a kind of showdown that could really tear this place apart." Up until now, Stanford's sit-ins have been reasonably short and remarkably bloodless.

"The first thing you do in a time of crisis is take a referendum," says the student president. Stanford is attuned to referenda as a method of avoiding violent confrontations. In the same election that Hayes topped his topless opponent, the student body condemned sit-ins by a margin larger than two to one. Students have been voting against coercion ever since. That did not prevent the sit-ins of spring 1969, but it has served to stabilize the campus after militant protests.

I'm convinced that an unarmed faculty-student peacekeeping force would be a helpful alternative to police on all campuses. And a regular system for taking referenda would also help—possibly as part of the registration procedure at the beginning of each term. A vote on campus controversies before any crisis would give both the administration and the dissidents a working notion of how students might react. Suppose, for instance, 80 percent of the student body voted for the removal of ROTC as a course for credit. A smart administration could proceed to honor that vote. Or suppose 80 percent of the students announced opposition to any student strike. A shrewd SDS would understand in advance that it could not count on strike support.

Denis Hayes' road is not so much middle as his own. He does not live on campus but in East Palo Alto (the nearest ghetto) with a black family. In return for chores, this white young man from Camas, Washington, helps pay for his room and board. When he is ill, says Hayes, "Mama takes care of me." Mama is the lady of the house, his employer.

What Hayes intends to work for is the perpetual schooling of everybody: "I have a naive faith that one day the United States is going to get over the idea of a general education in the university and that the whole society will be structured as an educational experience. I talk to alums—two years out of here and they've stopped studying anything. Well, the old idea of a school producing a western gentleman is silly. A good school can only produce a student."

The typical Stanford student is a creature who began college life at the upper middle. More than 40 percent of the freshmen come from families earning more than $20,000 a year. Nine out of 10 students intend to extend their educations beyond the bachelor's degree and into graduate work. Stanford is one of the 10 most difficult schools to enter in the United States, accepting only one applicant in five.

But, with all its socio-academic status, Stanford is not a cloistered refuge for the rich. It has an extraordinary proportion of people ready to work at street level. It sent more white students to the Deep South in 1964 to help black voter-registration than any other school. More Stanford kids participated in the Oakland Induction Center protests of 1967 than Berkeley students. Stanford has always had an extremely high percentage of Peace Corps volunteers.

The Tresidder Coffee House is one of the spaces that sets Stanford apart from other schools. It's a simple room furnished with old wooden tables and candlelight, serving espresso and fresh fruit and ices. The menu is scrawled across a blackboard. The managers and serving people are students. The entertainment is live.

During finals week, the Coffee House is a place to vent steam right on campus. Sam McGowan plays stride piano and Norm Cross accompanies him on guitar. They harmonize vocals, the black pianist and the white guitarist. Sam came to Stanford with a company from Studio Watts to do a play; he has stayed in Palo Alto to attend a nearby junior college until he can qualify for the university. Norm is a sophomore at Stanford; he plays for the pleasure and the pin money.

Tonight, the room is full. McGowan-Cross do *People Got to Be Free*, and that rock integration anthem inspires a few couples to start dancing in front of the serving counter. A girl in tights and a serape brings Cokes up to the performers between numbers, a soft-drink switch on the Joe E. Lewis ritual in Vegas.

Sam swings into *Don't You Know the Sound of a Man Workin' on a Chain*, and a few students halfway back in the room begin to stomp rhythm with their feet. Then the musicians chant *Baby, I Need Your Lovin'*, and a tall black student leaps onto one of the tables with a candle in his hand to perform a frantic solo dance interpretation while kids throughout the room start banging

102

their hands as background. The set breaks at midnight and this room is full of sweat and glee and good feelings. I look around and realize that this is the first campus I've visited where white and black students still sit at the same tables with each other. The new black-imposed apartheid hasn't yet happened here.

But there is one blond boy sitting by himself under a surrealistic painting in the corner. He's oblivious to the music and the noise and the modern dance. He has a book in his hands, something about geophysics, and he's able to concentrate even while the world quakes around him.

Dr. John Black is the head of Stanford's counselling center and a clinical psychologist who's been trying to stay abreast of what bothers students. In one of his seminar courses, Black asked undergraduates how they might change their behavior if they knew they had only six more months to live. He has saved some of the answers:

"I think I would stop worrying about myself and turn to others."

"For one thing, I would center my being in the present rather than always worrying about the future. I would spend less time breathing in and more time breathing out—more outgoing, more extroverted, a hell of a lot more trusting. I think I'd like it."

"I would become more giving, more loving and through that change I would hope to conquer some of the gnawing loneliness that permeates life so completely."

Only one student faced finality with greed: "I'd rape society for all it's worth."

Dr. Black sees Stanford kids as becoming ever more preoccupied with existential questions: that confirms a national survey of freshmen which indicated that the two chief undergraduate ambitions were to develop a meaningful philosophy of life and to help other people in difficult situations.

Two categorical pieces of graffiti near White Plaza, the Stanford free speech area:

"EDUCATION IS THE DESTRUCTION OF INNOCENCE."

"NONE OF US IS INFALLIBLE—NOT EVEN THE YOUNGEST OF US."

Soto House is the residence hall that caters to supposedly creative students. Just before the evening meal, the Soto living room is a sort of a circus. A young man plays Chopin on the piano, his long brown hair almost touching the keys as he hunches over trying to hear his own music. Two girls on a couch sing the Beatles' *Hey Jude* at each other. And two boys offer an exhibition of Indian hand-wrestling, struggling between the living room and the lobby.

Coeducational housing came to Stanford in 1967, starting with a few dorms that sheltered men and women who shared particular academic interests.

The experiment proved so successful and so relaxed that Dr. Joseph Katz, associate director of Stanford's Institute for the Study of Human Problems, was soon able to reassure the university and the parents about what happens in mixed housing. Boys and girls who occupy common living rooms and dining tables, said Katz, begin to treat each other more like brothers and sisters and less like enemies or lovers. He even suggested the new arrangement might tend to produce "a partial moratorium on sex."

A Stanford fraternity jumped into the residential revolution. Having dropped their old national affiliation, the men of Lambda Nu decided to become a coeducational club with memberships for both sexes. Now the old brothers and the new sisters—each in a separate wing—are living happily under one roof.

In 1969, another fraternity tried to retain its national charter and rent surplus living space to women. Phi Gamma Delta was talking to the university and to its alumni about taking in female boarders. The unprecedented application has survival implications along with sociological ones. Like other ex-strongholds of the fraternity system, Stanford is gradually losing its Greek-letter organizations. New social groupings, including coed dorms and off-campus apartment houses, are replacing the lure of a secret male society.

The Phi Gamma Deltas, for instance, have a handsome new post-and-beam house on campus with room for 51 resident bodies. But there are only 44 residents right now, making the cost of fraternity living quite expensive for the present members. President Jim Greer admits that many potential brothers prefer to live elsewhere. Phi Gam must either lower its selection standards or take in roomers to fill the house.

In the old days, belonging to a fraternity was a student status symbol. Nowadays, it can be a hindrance. "Being in a house has taken on a kind of onus," admits Phi Gam Fred Lonsdale.

"If you wore a pin around here for five minutes," agrees one of the brothers sitting around the living room fireplace, "you'd be subject to ridicule. Our rule is to keep your pin in your wallet. At Stanford, you probably have less chance to date, to meet all the women, if you're in a fraternity. And in certain courses, you hate to fill out the blank marked residence because you know damn well the professor is gonna dump on you for being a Greek."

Even inside the organization, fraternity life is not the same. "You used to be able to call up the house at 3 a.m.," says a member with a handlebar mustache, "and tell anybody who answered that you were in trouble—somebody would show up immediately. Now, if a good friend doesn't happen to pick up the phone, you're just not gonna get any help."

Rituals don't hold, either. "We used to have penalties if a guy didn't attend meetings," says Jim Greer. "That's out. Now we have to give door prizes to get people to come." Some members claimed the doxology before dinner offended their moral principles, so the Phi Gams have quit that, too.

The only time Phi Gamma Delta observes all the old customs is when one of the national field representatives pays the chapter a visit. Then members rush to the book of secrets and memorize all the proper incantations. The national, says Jim Greer, doesn't understand that colleges have changed and that crosscountry allegiances are no longer built on exclusive social clubs. "All we get from the national," he complains, "are bills and a magazine."

Two outraged alums have already told the Phi Gams that having resident girls would violate the basic tenets of fraternity living. That argument means little to the modern members. But the university itself has frowned on the idea of nonmembers living amidst a national organization. One day, this Stanford chapter may also decide to disaffiliate itself and go its own way, coeducational.

Graffiti outside of Encina Hall, scene of the spring sit-in: "REVOLUTION NOW."
And in a separate scrawl next to it: "YEAH, PAY LATER."

The committee for the Study of Education at Stanford, SES, meets during finals week. Nine members—six professors and three students—sit in a conference room in the engineering building

105

and work up their recommendations for a new kind of university. They've been sitting for day-long sessions for more than two years now, sharing box lunches and arguing with each other on a first name basis. The only easy way to recognize a professor is at the collar level—most faculty members still wear ties.

SES, under Vice Provost Herbert Packer, is now studying graduate education. It has already completed its undergraduate proposals which include such innovations as: allowing students to design their own majors; adding a reading period to each academic term; small seminars for freshmen; unlimited pass-fail grading; independent study for all students after their freshmen year.

The SES recommendations for undergraduates are subject to discussion by the student body and to approval by the faculty. They stand a good chance of being adopted.

But for Stanford and for all of us, maybe SES' most important contributions are in approach as well as substance. In the course of thrashing out proposals, the students and professors have had to define for themselves what a university is about. Some of their published definitions flirt with eloquence. For instance:

"The word 'education' comes from the Latin verb *educere* meaning 'to lead forth.' To lead does not mean to compel, or to pull. It means quite simply what it says. Education is a continuous process of discovery, beginning with man's first day and ending only when his mind closes in on itself and can find or conceive nothing new . . .

"Three things seem to follow. First, education cannot be limited by hours or years; it cannot be confined to time spent in a classroom. Secondly, education must be the concern of the student himself, self-willed and in large measure self-directed. It can never be compelled nor can knowledge be impressed on a mind unwilling to learn, if it is to be more than indoctrination. This leads to our third point: every student offers a new and untried hope that our imperfect world may be changed, that our understanding of ourselves and our environment may be increased by whatever imagination and creativity he can bring to his endeavors."

I wonder how many public schools, college or lower, proceed to educate from that student-centered perspective. They may offer lip service to ideas about untried hope but there are too many regulations to revise, too many red tapes to cut.

A public school, such as a wing of the University of California, must answer to a chancellor and a president and a governor and

106

a Board of Regents and a legislature and an electorate. Some of those overseers, especially the elected ones, are not exactly responsive to restructuring institutions for individual learners.

A private university, of course, has its own trustees to placate and many trustees at many private schools are more obsessed with improving the physical plant than improving the life of the mind. But private university trustees can be persuaded. Privately. They do not have to prove their political muscle in front of television cameras. They don't have frightened constituents to appease before the next election. They don't have to explain their policies in terms tax-burdened property owners will agree to.

The private schools are in a position to experiment. A privileged position. They can offer the public some valuable examples to follow.

The silent radical is a creature I first met at Palo Alto. He fits the Stanford tensions between traditional social manners and radical social motion. He's a bright student who cannot associate with organized radicals although he sees justice in most of their complaints.

"Let me lay my trip on you about why I'm going to Stanford," says a short, nervous boy while we walk across campus from the old Memorial Church to the new library. "I'm basically apolitical. When some kids say college is irrelevant, I don't care. Knowledge for the sake of knowledge is fine by me. But I've got these things that are tearing my brains out at the same time. My country is doing things I just can't approve of. So I talk to the SDS and they don't show me any logic. Just about every SDS member I've met, I've hated. And yet I agree with their demands. Some way, some other way, I've got to get involved. I'm not in school to avoid the draft. I've already turned in my card although I haven't told people about it. It's funny, I guess. I won't join the army and I can't join SDS."

Eckhard Schulz, a graduate student in engineering, is a vocal moderate. Stanford now has hundreds of them, collected in an organization called the Coalition for an Academic Community that includes conservatives and middle-roaders. If the silent radicals stay out of activism because they're repulsed by SDS, the vocal moderates have a similar problem. They're forced *into* activism because they're repulsed by SDS.

Schulz meets me for breakfast, a clean-cut, medium-sized man

107

who never had any intention of becoming involved until he went to pay his rent last year. "I'd forgotten the housing bill," he says, "and I went over to the Old Union with my check. I couldn't get in." The radicals were having a sit-in.

So Schulz went to a mass student body meeting instead and found himself arguing against coercive tactics. The television newsmen put a camera on him and suddenly Eckhard Schulz, the European-born married graduate student, was in politics. He was an activist. The next day, the press was expecting him to talk at the marathon meeting and so he became a spokesman.

"The average person comes here to study," says Schulz. "But a few malicious students are determined to cause any disturbance, any uproar they can. They sit around waiting to put a stick in the spokes and when they see a chance, they do it. I'm militantly opposed to militancy—and to force. I don't want an excess of disorder because I'm equally afraid of an excess of order."

Schulz is also a believer in referenda—as a way of proving to nonradical students that they are not alone. The inability to pay his rent has changed his whole life: "I'll finish my graduate work but I'm not sure any more what I'll do with it. I know now that I won't be standing in a laboratory somewhere."

Philip Taubman, a junior with curly hair and an easy smile, wrote the student handbook for the incoming Freshmen of 1968-69. After documenting the sit-in of the previous spring—all Stanford sit-ins seem to happen in the spring—Taubman wound up offering advice: "Going to Stanford means infinite experience. Each new student will live four unique years, most never getting too excited about a judicial structure or an administrative decision. You may be one. Stanford is not a hotbed of radicalism. It's not in its nature, or ours. But Stanford is waking up and ferment is growing on campus. It can be avoided. We ask only that you know it's there."

Phil Taubman leans toward the political left but he keeps one foot planted in the center, as a point of reference, as a base for progress. At lunch the day before the last finals, the history major says, "There are several institutions in this country that can be used to keep ideas competitive and changing. One is big business. Another is government. These are the same institutions many students despise; but I think they have a shortsighted view."

Taubman wants to shake up the Establishment. He also wants an enlightened Establishment to be there when the shaking is

108

done, with a new system committed to serving the needs of this new society.

If Stanford gets through its own constant examinations without serious violence, then it can be among the most usable of all institutions. By testing itself, this private school may yet be public education's best friend.

UCLA:
The Humanity Gap

I've been going to UCLA ever since moving to California a decade ago. I've gone there as an extension student, an art appreciator, a theater patron, a panel member and a great admirer of green spaces abloom with pretty girls. Culturally and visually, the campus in Westwood is good for what ails adulthood.

I think of the 50-year-old university as a superb neighbor whose tools I borrow and whose properties I enjoy. I'm not alone in exploiting those 400 nearby acres that cultivate scholarship and produce plenty of brains for picking. The citizens of no other city have gained more from having a public university in their midst than the people of Los Angeles have gained from UCLA. Maybe the citizens of no other city needed one so much—especially in the days when Southern California deserved to be called a cultural desert.

So I went to the University of California at Los Angeles feeling like an old friend, forgetting for a moment that a friend is usually spared the details of family arguments. That kind of forgetting may partly explain why we outside adults are surprised when any college erupts these days. We've always thought of school as nicely planted places of learning where nasty things are not allowed to happen. We've rarely heard about the inside fights until after a campus has exploded. Then we start talking about ungrateful children who don't appreciate what their elders have done for them.

This time, I went specifically to hang around, to audit my way among 28,000 students and discover what UCLA is like for its full-time citizens. My appreciation of the place became more complicated as my perspective changed. In one sweltering school day I attended a rally concerning white racism, a demonstration over table grapes, two unusually dull lectures in the social sciences, a rock concert and a discussion in the Institute of Government and Public Affairs. These were all inside events—as opposed to performances for visitors.

Wherever I went, students were complaining. Complaining about bigotry in the community, complaining about irrelevance in the curriculum, complaining about lack of student power. Most of all, they were complaining about each other, claiming that nobody cares enough to make change. At the end of the day, I went up to relax in the ballroom of the Student Union, a space the size of a football field full of Naugahyde chairs and sleeping bodies. Next to me sat a boy with long hair and torn blue jeans, showing more of his knees than his face. As he fell into the chair, he exhaled a scatological four-letter word in one long breath to no one in particular. I introduced myself and asked if anything was bothering him.

"Them," he said, pointing a dirty finger at the students drowsing or studying in the ballroom. "Around here, it seems like lethargy is the best policy. I just came from a lousy meeting and I'm sick of talking about what to do with them. The administration claims it talks to everybody. The radicals talk to themselves. The faculty talks to nobody. It isn't the movement that drives students wild; it's goddam size and goddam loneliness." The humanity gap in a high-density society.

This is a perfect morning as I drive down Beverly Glen Canyon toward the campus. The wind has blown the fog out of the Los Angeles Basin, and the sunlight is bright enough to make wet leaves shine. I pick up two hitchhikers in the canyon, a young man and a young woman, each carrying a separate load of books. On the way to school, they chatter about the scandal in the Italian Department. Some teaching assistants are accused of grading students on the basis of cash or sexual favors. With blood running on other campuses, UCLA is fortunate to have such an old-fashioned controversy—hanky-panky in the Romance Languages.

I park in the multi-level garage behind the Dickson Art Center, one of five nonteaching buildings at a school which has to provide almost as much space for vehicles as bodies.

A funny thing is happening in Dickson Plaza near the sculpture garden. A woman stands in the center of the walkway wearing what looks to be a red stocking cap. But the cap, instead of flopping to the side of her head, soars all the way to the roof of the two-story Art Gallery where another woman is wearing the other end of the same red hat. Students walk underneath without stopping; some of them don't even look.

I ask the lady at ground level what she's doing and she in turn refers me to a man on a nearby bench. He's sitting under a tall black hat, talking to a student while beaming at the disinterested passersby. He tells me his name is Jim Byars and that he's the artist who conceived this 100-foot hat for two. It's a stunt to advertise an art show opening, but nobody is even inquiring.

"They're scared," says the undergraduate who is helping Byars install the exhibit. "Scared, hostile or blasé; we have a lot of each."

The air is so clean I keep walking through the new North Campus, across the matching lawns between Architecture and Music, and over to the miraculous circular fountain outside of Knudsen Hall. Maybe it really isn't a fountain at all, because fountains gush outward and this one sucks inward. A stone circle encloses a bed of large, smooth rocks. Water flows from the circumference of the circle, over the rocks, toward a large hole just off the center.

Six students are sitting on the outer rim, watching the water rush into the hole. I join them and decide this is the perfect work of art for a down-looking, inward-staring generation. There are some students on some days who wade into the inverted fountain and stand in the hole, hoping to become part of a cycle that is smooth on the surface and turbulent at its core.

The Upstairs is supposed to be where the multiversity undergraduate can meet the multiversity professor on informal, extracurricular terms. A large lounge atop Kerckhoff Hall has been partitioned into sitting rooms, and every day an impressive assortment of professorial volunteers take hourly turns making themselves available for discussions.

A few students started the Upstairs last year, thinking it would be a happy answer to complaints about the impersonal nature of a commuters' school where lectures are in large halls and professorial office hours, like doctors' office hours, are usually by appointment or emergency request. The students who started it were worried whether teachers would give their time. The professors would and did.

UCLA Coalition spokesman, Gordy Alexander

UCLA at lunchtime

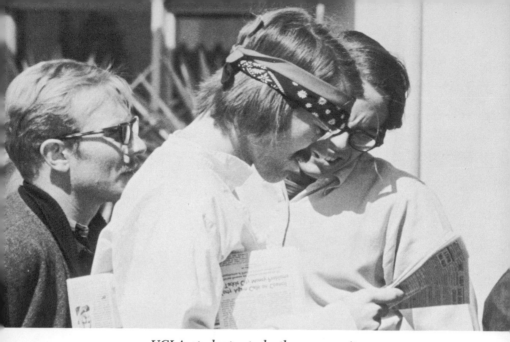

UCLA students study the community

Street theater on UCLA campus

The trouble is that students haven't been giving their time. The situation is a little like UC-Berkeley's ombudsman: in 1968 several Berkeley undergraduates decided that students needed a sympathetic ear, someone between the administration and the kids, someone who could offer advice or consolation. The school agreed, a teacher volunteered, an office was set up, and then nobody came. The ombudsman was so unbusy that his sponsors developed galloping cases of guilt. They finally asked friends to make up problems and carry them to the ombudsman so he would feel needed.

Samuel Surace, sociologist, and Robert Griffin, historian, are the Upstairs authorities this morning. Only three students arrive, so the teachers combine forces to make a conversational handful. One of the students is an Upstairs organizer, and she's embarrassed by the turnout. Surace tells her that he's not surprised; he's been disappointed before.

The bearded sociologist says that many members of the faculty are really lonely for student contact. He keeps his door open during office hours so that people will feel free to drop in, with or without prior notice. "But hardly anybody shows up. One man did stop by to complain about the way I dress. He wanted to know why I always wear a tie and so I told him I happen to feel comfortable with a tie."

Last quarter Surace invited 360 students to drop in for one-to-one conversations with him. About 40 students eventually accepted the invitation, and about half of them used the time to discuss personal problems.

"Some students tell me incredible things," Surace says. "For instance, some are ashamed to go out and be seen with their parents—especially on weekends." Maybe, he suggests, there is a kind of fear operating; kids are afraid of publicly showing that they need or enjoy adult company. And that sort of fear could be what keeps the Upstairs as empty as it is.

A young woman who has been fidgeting with her notebook finally speaks: "Have we covered this topic thoroughly?" she asks Surace. "I came here to see you, to learn about your background. I'm basically interested in working in sociology and since I'm older than most students, I want to meet people in the field and learn the ropes, professionally."

The other two students wince, but Surace explains politely that he was a jazz musician who became tired of a suitcase life.

115

Teaching is his second profession, after a career playing bass and guitar. "Sociology," he confesses, "attracts the undisciplined human being." It's a field where people search for themselves by learning about other people.

The hour ends. The three students and the two professors offer extravagant thanks to one another for having attended the Upstairs, all of them apologizing for the size of the crowd.

For a week, I keep coming back to see whether the Upstairs is going to flourish. But I finally give up hope—maybe even an informal schedule is too much structure for modern students.

Professors aren't the only creatures feeling neglected on campus these days. White students go around worrying why black students snub them. Many of the 700 black students at UCLA have consciously and conspicuously segregated themselves from their classmates and this separation has a wholly unsettling effect on white liberals.

As I walk from Kerckhoff Hall toward Royce Hall, I overhear a white girl complaining to a black girl that she was ignored by a few black kids in one of her classes. "Well, personally," says the black girl, smiling and patting her friend on the back, "I always go out of my way to be nice to white people—just to prove to them that they're still wanted."

At noon, the rally in Meyerhoff Park is supposed to demonstrate UCLA's radical solidarity with the radical movements at San Francisco State College. Several organizations, including the local chapters of the SDS, the BSU and the Black Panthers, are sponsoring guest speakers from San Francisco and leaders from the home campus.

Almost 300 people sprawl on the sloping lawn in front of Kerckhoff. This is a peculiarly confined, uneven area for a free speech platform. UCLA has at least 10 grander, greener spaces. Why, I wonder, doesn't the university have its open forum in a place that could accommodate a massive gathering of students?

William Stanton, a San Francisco State faculty member, is introduced and begins a tirade about San Francisco president S. I. Hayakawa, calling him "the megalomaniac who runs State with a tam-o'-shanter on his head—apparently to cover the hole in it." The applause is sporadic. What's significant is that this same man has been all over California delivering the same message.

116

The conservatives who scream that "outside agitators" are popping up on every campus are partly correct. By the time I attended UCLA on my campus tour, I had seen the same face at four or five schools. But conservatives are wrong when they claim this is all part of some conspiracy. In truth, it's a case of common inter-campus passion coupled with the jet age. Cheap fares and convenient schedules make it possible for audiences in Northern and Southern California to hear the same speeches from the same spokesmen almost simultaneously.

As Stanton goes on to blame police for inciting violence on his campus, a handful of pickets from UCLA's moderate-to-right Thomas Jefferson Club circle the crowd. "WHAT'S CONSTRUCTIVE ABOUT DESTRUCTION?" reads one of their signs. A few radical students heckle the pickets. An equal number applaud the pickets. This audience is more curious than committed. The lawn is good for a lethargic lunch, and several people are eating sandwiches out of cellophane wrappers. The rally is just an added attraction.

John Huggins, representing the UCLA Black Panthers, is the next speaker. He's a thin, intense young man wearing a black turtleneck sweater, black glasses, natural hairdo and trimmed beard. "I believe," says Huggins, "that education should teach a person how to survive, how to live in his environment. We're dealing with the survival of people who've been brought to this country and brutalized."

Huggins is an effective orator but Thomas Robischon, a professor of education, seems to speak for more of the audience when he takes the platform and suggests, "The alternative to violence is a university—is being what we pretend to be as human beings."

A boy standing near me in the crowd puts his arm around a heavy blond girl and says, "Yeah, but if you're really human, you also have to go to jail once in a while."

She laughs and answers, "Okay—after you."

Jail is an alternative to college now, along with the army. Most male students seriously consider prison as one of the ways to beat the draft. Although few young men carry their Vietnam objections that far, uncertainty about service is a well-bottom cause of the unrest that spills out in violent demonstrations or alienation.

"The draft is almost like a hair shirt," says Les Rothenberg, a UCLA law school graduate who has been counselling students

117

about their military situations. "It has enormous short-range implications for these guys. Literally life or death. Maybe it sounds silly but a lot of them—when they're really honest with you—are convinced that if they get inducted they're gonna die.

"I get all types," continues Rothenberg, who has the reassuring smile of an unflusterable psychologist, "from the kids who are going to Canada to the ones who want to blow up buildings. They're amazingly candid about almost everything, even homosexuality. The sad thing is that the guy who comes in today with a legitimate homosexual claim has a real problem. The Induction Center has learned to be very suspicious, especially in Los Angeles, where they're dealing with so many actors."

The draft also affects women students. "The girls seem to be more aggressive now," says Rothenberg, "partly because boys are afraid of committing themselves. Some women decide to forget about trying to get married and they go into careers until the men come back from the service. Even the faculty has its draft troubles; professors worry about giving flunking grades and causing somebody to lose his student deferment."

Rothenberg has met one student who went barefoot for a whole summer to build calluses on his feet and thereby stand above the height limit—but the limit was raised even while the boy was blistering. He's seen a young man who posed for pornographic pictures hoping to show evidence of unfitness for service—but the army doesn't ask for snapshots. And he's talked to a desperate man who planned to join the police force in preference to military service—but that may leave everybody less protected.

One of the inequities of the draft is that college students have the guile and the money to invest in various forms of evasion. One of the simplest and most expensive is a set of orthodontic braces; the military doesn't take men while their teeth are supposedly being straightened.

The *Daily Bruin* is UCLA's student newspaper, often angering both radicals and campus conservatives. That means the *Bruin* is usually a pretty honest piece of journalism, although adults in Los Angeles will find the *Bruin's* middle position far to the left of what passes for liberal on the outside.

Mike Levett, a thin law student who talks easily enough to be a monologist, is the *Bruin* editor this year, and he's an everyday authority on why UCLA has remained relatively calm while other major schools have been in violent trouble. We meet in Levett's apartment just before midnight, after the newspaper has been sent to the printers for another day. I've brought wine because Levett doesn't drink whisky, but Mike can't find a corkscrew and so we sit and talk soberly until 2 a.m. about a school where grade point averages still count.

Levett sprawls on the couch and starts talking: "I think there are a growing number of students trying to answer the question of what they're doing—trying to find a place for themselves in this world. But they aren't particularly interested in doing it at the university. They *are* attending the university and getting their grades and writing their papers, but they're doing other things outside.

"We've always had a lot of activists at UCLA who were never active while they were on campus. They just don't give a damn about this particular campus. Look at the stupid little things, like graffiti. When they build new buildings and put up a construction fence at almost any school, kids splash paint or graffiti all over the thing. But you don't see that here." He's right. For better or worse, UCLA is one of the tidiest schools in the country.

So, Levett asks, "Are we supposed to complain because nobody's painting around a construction zone when, more important, we really don't have to demonstrate for things like more black professors? As soon as we run up against a real issue here, all of a sudden Chuck Young, the chancellor, comes out and says something like, 'Before any problems arise, here is my proposal for . . .' Meanwhile, people are rioting on some other campus over exactly that issue."

The UCLA administration in recent years, first under Franklin Murphy and lately under Charles Young, has indeed attempted to anticipate undergraduate fury and cool it before violence. The two reasons most often cited for calm in Westwood are administration foresight and commuting fatigue. But Levett has another theory that makes sense:

"The kids who wanted to be most active on campus went to Berkeley in the first place. If you were liberal and you were a little different, you went up there. Anybody who wanted to get involved in activities, leftwing or social, tended toward Berkeley, even when I was in high school. That place attracted the kind of kids who were going to take part in the Free Speech Movement.

"UCLA never did. Because UCLA was a school—a nice school

119

to go to, a good school, a pretty campus. But Berkeley had the reputation that would attract the active people—active politically, sexually, psychedelically, religiously. Certainly it has more of a reputation now and that reinforces the difference. One reason why UCLA hasn't exploded is that the kids who might have exploded it went someplace else instead."

Levett fights student lethargy because he wants his schoolmates to be active in the larger community. His policy is to make the *Bruin* reflect more than the campus proper, more than the upper suburb in which UCLA sits: "Westwood is not the college town for UCLA. Los Angeles is. I think people forget that you can go to Sunset Strip as easily as Westwood Boulevard. Everybody drives—it's no big thing. I don't think there's such a thing as a campus community any more and if there was I think I'd be the first one to attempt to destroy it. I don't like ivory towers anywhere. And so if I say relevance, I mean what's relevant to the whole L.A. area."

There is, of course, a danger when students insist on participating outside. "When you decide you have to knock down the ivory tower and throw the university into the community, then you have to realize the community's eyes will be on you. There isn't any way to hide behind the old institution," says the 24-year-old editor who may graduate into politics. "And while we have to accept that, then it also becomes incumbent upon the legislature and the government to take over some of the responsibility to protect academic inquiry, protection the ivory tower used to provide."

Rosalio Munoz, the UCLA student body president, sits in his private office near the Upstairs in Kerckhoff Hall. A poster of Che Guevara and a picture of the Zapata brothers decorate his wall, gentle reminders that Ross Munoz is a Mexican-American, an advocate and a system-shaker as well as a campus politician. He was instrumental in starting UCLA's Experimental College before running for office and he has been a champion of minority causes on campus.

But today, small, soft-spoken Ross Munoz wipes his thick glasses and says, "Things have been pretty dead around here. I kind of have a guilt feeling because we haven't gotten moving lately. People seem to be at a loss to know how to accomplish anything constructively—all they seem to want to do is fight Ronald Reagan." Ross blames editor Levett, in part, for the inactivity. The *Bruin* is accused of downplaying campus questions by concentrating on statewide issues such as the governor and the Board of Regents.

Ross has been trying, as president, "to get involved in the system and see how far we can push it." This year there have been many more undergraduates involved in joint committees with the faculty and the administration. "But students," Ross says, "especially the younger ones, don't really know what they want from the university. The natural instinct is for the school to baby-sit the kids. The faculty doesn't really deal with the students as human beings. But, hell, the students don't think of themselves as human beings."

Ross wants UCLA to forget about insisting on degree requirements and majors until a student has had a chance to know the place for himself, to sample what a university with 14 schools and 70 buildings has to offer. The student president grew up juggling two cultures—the Chicano barrio in which he lived and the academic world in which his father started teaching when Ross was an adolescent. "I'll tell you the truth," he says, "I'm lost right now. So many forces are pushing me in ways that would make my life easier. But then there are responsibilities I have to people back there. Sometimes I think history is a nightmare from which I'm trying to awaken."

The activistic, left-leaning organizations at UCLA have glued themselves together as The Coalition. The activistic right-leaning and moderate groups have amalgamated as the Free Student Union. This afternoon it's the FSU's turn to have a rally at Meyerhoff Park. About 100 people are sitting on the grass as a folk singer strums his own accompaniment to *Red Wine Is a Friend to the Poor*. Then he gets up and goes away, and I'm not even sure he was part of the program.

There's an American Flag on the platform and a group of students wearing blue armbands—a symbol of antiradicalism imported from San Francisco State—gather around the microphone stand. Some of them have signs, including one placard drawn so that the angular "S's" in SDS are crossed with horizontal "S's" to become swastikas.

"We're here to show support for an academic environment,"

121

says Charles Stephens, the former president of UCLA's Thomas Jefferson Club, "and our opposition to violence, vilification and vandalism."

A freaky looking boy in red flowing pants, wide flowered tie and windblown serape begins to lead a few hecklers less than 50 feet from the speaker. Charles Stephens, a tall, clean-cut blond, first ignores the hecklers and then smiles and shouts, "Yes, those are the tactics, those are the tactics."

"Yeah, violence," yells one of the hecklers, laughing.

Stephens introduces a speaker from Long Beach State and then introduces Larry Labovitz, San Fernando Valley State's student president who has tried to organize his campus against militancy. Labovitz is known to UCLA. The hecklers start singing *For He's a Jolly Good Fellow.* Stephens grabs the mike and compares the hecklers to Hitler youth and Stalinists. The audience applauds Stephens.

Labovitz begins, "I see we have my fan club here today." Then he proceeds to attack SDS for using "the big lie," for enraging people with screams of "kill the pig," and for turning their organization into the "Sandbox Dictator Society." In the couple of months since I saw Larry operate at his own school, he's become a polished performer, a veteran of several campus speaking engagements. The anti-militants also travel the free speech circuit and I wonder whether the conservatives would condemn them as outsiders.

Chuck Reid, a UCLA student, follows Labovitz and the heckling becomes steadier, almost a cacophonic Greek chorus.

Stephens comes back on the platform to open a question-answer session but first addresses himself to the crowd: "I do not talk of love and call people pigs . . . These people," and he waves at his antagonists, "talk of expanded educational opportunities, but they close campuses down." The crowd has now swelled to nearly 400 people as passersby have stopped to hear the argument. There are more neutrals and there are more hecklers.

As soon as the questioning starts, the radicals sing "We are not alone" to the tune of *We Shall Overcome.* And then about 20 of them surge toward the microphone. Some student throws a paper wad into the crowd and one of the radicals yells, "Bomb." I hurry up front where kids with blue armbands have become a human wall against the hecklers. A tall graduate student from the FSU side rushes in between the two groups, throws out his arms as if being crucified and begs for a reconciliation, pleading "the nobility of man." A banner suddenly appears from a window on the top floor of Kerckhoff. "THIS ROOM IS LIBERATED," it says.

Just when I expect someone to throw the first punch, students break up into small, separate argumentative clusters on the grass. As they debate this way, facing each other, they all become reasonable creatures. Their common bond—student age and student status—reasserts itself. I remember that a similar confrontation at Pomona College became productive as soon as people stopped marching or shouting through bullhorns and started talking to each other.

The six or seven small discussion groups go on for about 15 minutes and then students begin to drift away. "We can go now," says one of the radical kids sarcastically. "Can't miss our one o'clock classes."

One of his friends turns to him: "Yeah, that's all. UCLA is Berkeley with mothers."

I walked away from the rally feeling optimistic about my old neighbor, the mammoth multiversity. I sat down at the in-gushing fountain and decided UCLA would probably solve its internal arguments if the resident scholars kept recognizing each other as family. Then I liberated my car from multistory parking structure "L" and headed for home.

A couple of hours later I turned on the radio for news. Two students had just been shot at UCLA. Both of them had died. One of them was John Huggins. And I had heard him saying in Meyerhoff Park only a few days earlier, "I believe an education should teach a person how to survive . . . ."

The announcer said the murders seemed to have been the result of a fight between two factions in the Black Students Union, after a meeting of that organization with representatives from the community.

Mike Levett was right. The ivory tower has been destroyed and nobody can hide behind the institution any more. Now UCLA, in its second half-century, has a tragedy to outgrow as well as a distinction to live up to.

BERKELEY:
'The Enemy is the Inhumanity...'

The University of California Berkeley, attracts the best-qualified students in the state. The University of California, Berkeley, staggers along as the campus with the most unrest in the state. The University of California, Berkeley, is an experience loved by its bright students—despite sit-ins, strikes and senseless violence.

If the educated adults of the State of California could accept those three statements, then they might begin to understand this student generation. And they might begin to realize that the troubles with students grew out of the troubles with us, the parents of the problem.

I came to Berkeley between emergencies, after the winter student strike of 1968 and before the spring student strike of 1969. But the campus seethes constantly, a perpetual stew of activism, idealism and impatience always just one incident, a random spark below the boiling point.

UCB is unlike every other school I visited because all of Berkeley is a city of students, with no clear separation between college and community. It is a mash of young people where a grown man looks and feels like a member of a minority group.

Signs saying, "Property of the Regents of the University of California," mark the campus borders. They also pock-mark the town; they're posted on parking lots and dormitory-apartment houses and other facilities that have spilled out of the original 1,200-acre preserve. I kept seeing the signs as I drove around town for 20 minutes trying to park. The municipal spaces were full. The University's spaces were also full. I finally pulled into one of the Regents'-owned lots and left my car there, squeezed illegally between an old tree and a new Mustang, an act of impatient frustration that would later earn me WARNING NOTICE 10443 on my windshield.

Telegraph Avenue supports bookstalls and record shops and coffee houses and clothing stores—all the retail services you would expect of a street that leads into the middle of academia. It also has beggars and drug dealers and hippies and informal philosophers—all the creatures that have come to be named "street people" in Berkeley. Some of them literally live outdoors, without a mailing address. In the summer of 1968, it was the street people and the students who staged a minor Paris riot along Telegraph. In 1969, it was the street people and the students who met the police head-on in the confrontation over the People's Park.

Telegraph Avenue smells. It has the incense smell of a Middle Eastern bazaar. It has the short order smell of Broadway in New York. It has the human body smell of Taiwan. I walked up the avenue marveling at the funny odors, the barefoot pedestrians, the costumes in the crowd. Part commerce, part carnival, Telegraph was busy in the mid-morning with more people along the sidewalk than any avenue west of Chicago.

Some of the Berkeley electricity is generated by this pedestrian traffic. You can actually hear the thump of human beings walking as you cross Bancroft Way to the university entrance. And the feeling of downtown flows right into the campus. I stopped to gawk at an apple stand on the sidewalk right near the student union. Kids were coming up to the street vendor and buying fresh fruit—10 cents an apple—to munch on the way to classes.

Young people lounged on the steps of the student union, talking and watching the human parade like village oldsters loafing in front of the town square courthouse. I walked by them and into the union. It's a new building with rectangular spaces and crisp contemporary furnishings; but students decorated the place with their presence. Their fringed jackets, frayed jeans and flowing hair covered the chairs and crannies like a sea of shag rugs. There were kids sprawled across couches, crouching on floors, squatting on stairways.

Suddenly, two dogs ran out from under a coffee table and I followed them outside to Ludwig's Fountain. The fountain, between the dining commons and Sproul Hall, was once named after a generous donor, just like other landmarks at other schools. It has been renamed, by the students, in honor of Ludwig, a beloved dog who spent his days playing there. The original Ludwig passed away but I saw six dogs splashing through the fountain spray that morning.

Dogs are a part of the everyday campus confusion, along with visiting children, wandering minstrels and street people. Adopting a stray animal has become important to the new morality—a proof that a person truly cares—and so thousands of UCB students are dog fanciers. The kids drop the animals off at the fountain when they go to classes.

There was a girl screaming "Beowulf, Beowulf, BAY-YO-WOOL-LUF," for a dog that had obviously run off during one of her courses. Another student took up her cry, half in sympathy, half for the fun of it. I interrupted him and asked if UCB's animal population was a problem. "It used to be worse," he said, petting his own Freudian beard. "They just passed a leash law on campus because there were 43 people bitten around here last year. The dogs are great but every now and then they get confused by the crowds or one of them is teased. Usually, they just play or swipe people's lunches."

I asked him whether the school would begin to enforce the new leash law and the student shrugged. "I suppose that depends," he said, "on what else they'll be enforcing this quarter. I'd hate to see the dogs go; they're kind of heroes. A couple of years ago there were a lot of them named after Bernard, you know, from the movie *You're a Big Boy Now.* Then last year we suddenly had a lot of 'Benjamins' after *The Graduate.*"

I spent the rest of that day wandering and discovering that Berkeley is full of other outdoor surprises.

The College of Environmental Design, for instance, had a peculiar legend lettered along four stories of one side. "GLA" it said on the top floor. "SSS" said the next floor, followed by "PRI" and then "SON." A student translated it as "Glass Prison" and explained that the mammoth letters referred to UCB's attempt to prevent campus suicides. When Wurster Hall was first built, it had open concrete balconies at several levels. But then people started leaping off the balconies and the school glassed them in. "You can't really stop someone from committing suicide," said the student, "you can only force him to go somewhere else."

Suicide is an unspoken worry at many campuses; at Berkeley, it is an everyday topic. The roof of the student union is locked from the inside at night because kids had used it as a jumping place. A couple of years ago, student Douglas Lummis wrote a prose poem about Barrows Hall: "In the basement is a computer installation. On the roof is a suicide platform . . . How do you

126

Hubert Lindsay, Berkeley soul-saver

Two spirits of Sproul Plaza

The Berkeley carnival at Sproul Plaza

respond when a body comes crashing down outside your classroom?"

There was a contradictory sign of life in front of Dwinelle Hall. A young man stood there playing Bach on the violin. He had all the surface trappings of a member of the vibration generation: black shirt and torn black pants, black hair combed out in electric coils, thick black mustache insulating the corners of his mouth. Yet there he was on the plaza, playing classical music and playing it beautifully.

Students and professors drifted in and out of his audience, the crowd rising and falling between 50 and 25 people. Many of the people tossed quarters into his open violin case on the pavement. Someone suggested that he earns his living this way, and I later learned that the campus is a stage for several strolling players who perform and pass the hat, a modern version of Renaissance street theater. Berkeley is full of music and conversation and city excitement. Some days it's even happy.

I also found a completely quiet place in the midst of human clamor. Strawberry Creek winds around and through the school. Behind Stephens Hall there's a magnificent glade of grass and great redwoods. I could collapse there and contemplate how difficult it must be to attend a school where there's a constant barrage, a continual assault upon the senses. Noon, of course, is the magical time. Most students are on campus, the rallies happen and the assaults intensify.

Noon is organization time at Sproul Plaza, when various campus groups unfold their bridge tables, like sidewalk merchants, and try to make converts by pamphlet, argument, petition. One day there were seven separate outfits lined up in front of Ludwig's Fountain: the Meher Baba League, named after the Indian mystic; the Science Students for Social Responsibility; the Young People's Socialist League; SWOP, a tutorial project; Campus Draft Opposition; the Students for a Democratic Society; and the University Glee Club. I was standing behind the lines listening when a girl suddenly ran between Glee Club and Young Socialists to grab a boy by the arm. He was apparently an old friend but new to Berkeley because she asked, "D'you like it here?" "I love it," answered the boy. "It's so crowded."

One noon the Black Panthers came to campus. That was probably the quintessence of my Berkeley experience because there

129

were three events happening at once around Sproul Plaza: an evangelical harangue, a country music concert, and a political rally. Let me try to re-create it, moving from south to north across the face of the student union.

Hubert Lindsay is up on a little box next to the apple vendor screaming, "Until God makes you righteous, you're filthy." Lindsay is neither a street person nor a faculty member. He's a middle-aged auctioneer who comes to campus almost every day to preach the gospel. His freckled face glows as red as the stripes on his shirt. Lindsay tells a gathering of some 70 students that they're doing the work of the devil. "C'mon you sinners," he yells.

And students yell back, using an assortment of philosophical arguments and four-letter words to upset him. UCB has its own undergraduate satanist and he's right up front quarreling with Hubert and saying: "Truth is that which is convenient."

It's obvious that the agnostic kids and the apostolic adult really love each other. The students come out to give Hubert his ration of sinners. And he offers the students a sense of tradition to battle. Like a marriage that thrives on combat, the evangelist is wedded to Berkeley. I'm told he even lends money to the kids for emergencies.

Less than 100 yards away, the Cleanliness and Godliness Skiffle Band is performing. The group consists of two guitars, harmonica, tambourine and a bass. The bass is a string attached to a bucket with a broom handle. They do folk melodies such as *How High's the Water, Mama?* and, like the virtuoso of the violin, they pass the hat to sustain their music. I don't much like country music but C&G play with obvious pleasure and some 100 students applaud.

The Panthers arrive to support Berkeley students involved in the Oakland Stop-the-Draft movement. The leader is Bobby Seale and he is resplendent in black coat and caracal hat, flanked by matching bodyguards. Seale addresses some 300 Berkeley students from the steps of Sproul Hall and says the Panthers will launch a campaign in the black community to support the students, "not because they're white but because we have a common enemy . . . The same grand jury that indicted Huey P. Newton indicted the Oakland Seven . . . If we can't understand that, then we're just jiving ourselves."

Seale, quoting from Eldridge Cleaver, suggests that liberation

130

of the black colony and revolution among white students make blacks and students logical allies. He winds up with a Panther litany: "All Power to the people. Black power to black people. Ho Chi Minh power to Ho Chi Minh. End the war in Vietnam. Power to the Vietnamese. And even some white people's power as long as they don't act like racists."

The audience loves it because Bobby Seale, in one rhetorical swoop, has made everything all right. He's laid the footings for a bridge between black and white, something many of these kids have been working for since the freedom rides. He's announced against the war, something these kids hate by political stance and personal fear. He's aligned his party against the university establishment, just by being here and speaking to students.

Many adult observers have said the student revolution grew out of an affluent society whose kids who had so many advantages and so many things they were spoiled—and so they turned to destruction for lack of a better adventure. I think there's a second step in logic. These affluent kids could afford to care about other people. They knew that their good fortune was not everybody's good fortune, and that black militants built a strong moral argument from a position of community weakness. The students have been trying to be on the black side for nearly a decade. But many black groups distrust well-to-do white students who haven't been oppressed. By becoming "revolutionaries," affluent students could suffer and provoke oppression. They could be recognized as losers when the majority society turned its wrath and weapons on *them*, as in the case of the Berkeley People's Park. I'm not sure the student rebels want to win as much as they want to prove their ability to suffer. And that may be why affluent radical students offer more negative protests than positive programs.

The Cleanliness and Godliness band comes over to offer a musical coda for the rally. As they thwack away on *Catch a Falling Star and Put It In Your Pocket*, a girl wearing a suede coat, eyeglasses and tights twirls a baton on the steps in a perfect parody of a drum majorette at a football game.

A tall, smiling, wavy-haired man has stood through the whole rally near the front rows of students. His name is Mario Savio and hardly anyone has paid attention to him. Mario Savio gave passion and voice to the Free Speech Movement at Berkeley in 1964, when American student activism really began. The troubles at Columbia, Harvard, Wisconsin and San Francisco State have

131

roots in what Savio was about. He was dismissed from school at the time but the FSM won its battle. The sadness, ever since, is that neither students nor administrators have known how to apply the virtues of free expression to the difficult business of peaceful reform.

In 1969, Savio lives quietly in Berkeley, with a wife and a child and a job in a Telegraph Avenue bookstore. He doesn't talk to the press. Students rarely talk to him; his nonviolent tactics seem old hat to a lot of them. The radical movement changes heroes with each graduating class. So Savio is an outsider who comes on campus to look and to learn.

Tom Hayden is one of the exceptions to the rule of a short active radical life. A founder of the SDS on the East Coast, Hayden gradually worked his way to Berkeley via confrontations at Columbia and the Chicago Democratic Convention.

Tom Hayden was hired to teach "The New American Revolution" by the Center for Participant Education, UCB's approved version of an experimental college. It was to be an extension of the course Eldridge Cleaver began in the fall of 1968, the one that caused all the furor over whether a lectern in a public university should be occupied by a Black Panther as teacher.

Hayden appeared for his first session in the ballroom of the student union, a small man with a modest mustache, little goatee and conventional sport shirt. He looked less revolutionary than most of the people who jammed the room. A little baby sitting on her father's shoulders began to cry. The baby's mother hauled the child outside while the father stayed for the lecture. Students sat in the aisles, stood in the rear. A few TV newsmen from San Francisco showed up to film the session but the audience objected to the cameras.

"One of the reasons I left the university many years ago," began Hayden, "was huge lectures like this." He talked easily and well, without a prepared text. Hayden rhetorically asked why revolution should be taught on a campus and then answered: "Because the question is central to the course . . . a matter of testing the openness of this institution—checking out whether you can study revolution for credit."

His first lecture would be an attempt to trace where the New Left came from, starting with the notion that after World War II a permanent military establishment emerged, to join with business and government as a triangulation of American power. The state became the chief employer for the private sector. "The values of private property, puritanism and hard work became irrelevant," said Hayden. "The values of militarism and racism became suicidal. And other values—democracy and humanism—became subversive . . . Because a collective society can't support the power of the community and the individual."

The new generation, continued Hayden, was born with material security and so it grew up searching for values beyond competition and money. Meanwhile, black people and other minorities were "getting up off their knees to take their destinies in their own hands." I looked around. Nobody sleeping, although Hayden's delivery was consciously cool and without any of the rising inflections of modern rabble rousers. The new movements among young whites and angry blacks, said Hayden, are movements that "have embodied the values that are subversive to this society." Democracy and humanism. "We're in a period of permanent instability and crisis," he concluded. The class applauded. The lecturer had not once advocated violence.

I went to a few other Participant Education courses. One was called Utopia and only 12 people showed up. They began by discussing their experiences with communes. "There's a whole lot of people who live together," said one pale blond girl, "and then the commune is destroyed because nobody washes the dishes."

A boy bragged that you can buy 100 pounds of brown rice for only $8 if you want to support a community cheaply. "That's really cool," answered a girl, "if you're freaky on brown rice."

I was fascinated by the instructor who insisted that the group agree on some minimal structure: "Like one class I was in," he said, "we all sat around and got stoned at the second meeting and the whole thing fell apart." But in that entire hour, the instructor never told the group his name.

The course called "Non-Violence and Social Change" was led by Peter Bergel, a gaunt, blond man who wore a headband and fondled his majestic nose during the seminar. He spoke quietly, firmly, almost messianically. He asked each of the 13 people in the room to explain what made them want to take the course. I especially liked Brock de Lappe's answer because it had to do with guns and guns have become a survival symbol among radicals.

133

Brock said he had been an SDS member at Colorado before he came to Berkeley. "I had projected the revolution, in my mind, to happen this summer and I didn't know what to do so I bought a gun and sat with it in my room. It was really a hassle in my skull. And then I put the gun away . . . and then I took it out one day . . . and I fired it. The day I first fired my gun I sold it. I knew I couldn't *use* it."

"Then what are you gonna do," asked another boy in the class, "when the pigs start beating your sister over the head?"

"I dunno," said de Lappe. "I guess that's why I'm here."

Bergel led them through a discussion of Ghandi and the theory that nonviolence is more than the absence of violence. It's the substitution of a positive value, of conflict resolution through *satyagraha*—which is a combination of truth, self-sacrifice and noninjury. Interesting: girls outnumbered men in the class by better than two to one. And there were no black students.

As preparation for Berkeley, I had asked reporter Sharon Wanglin to poll UCB students on the subject of violence and demonstrations. She interviewed a cross-campus sample of 285 kids, more than half of whom said they had participated in at least one demonstration. Of the 151 students who had demonstrated, 54 said they would use violence when it seemed necessary. Of the 134 students who said they had not yet demonstrated, 21 felt that violent dissent might be acceptable, while 57 would stop at nonviolent disobedience and 55 others would draw a line somewhere between persuasion and passive resistance.

That poll was taken before the bloodshed over People's Park. After the Park horrors an undergraduate named Richark Marks would write home to his parents: "So now there are troops and guns and injuries and fear because the university has decided to show its authority. Such a waste of valuable resources. Such a wall of inhumanity being constructed around the laws, rules, and regulations of our society. I really despair at the thought of the future of this university. This incident strikes closer to home than any other since I've been here. The enemy isn't the war, or the military-industrial complex, or racism. The enemy is the inhumanity."

Students Larry Magid and Dave Kemnitzer are two instigators of Berkeley's CPE, the Center for Participant Education. Both are extra-articulate and portly. Magid organized the Eldridge Cleaver course. Kemnitzer wrote CPE's credo this year.

I invited them to dinner one night because they are veterans of the Berkeley wars and because their appetites for conversation even exceed their appetites for food. Kemnitzer wanted to go to Jack's, one of the oldest and fanciest restaurants on the San Francisco side of the Bay. I looked at their clean but unbusinesslike costumes without saying anything—let Jack's cast the first stone.

We must have looked menacing when we arrived because as soon as our party came into the brightly-lit restaurant, a whole roomful of people stopped eating to stare at us. Their faces went napkin-white, bleached by fear or surprise. The headwaiter came over and semi-scared and semi-belligerent, said, "Anything we can do for *you?*" I told him we wanted a table. He invoked a necktie rule. I started to go. Then he offered us a private dining room upstairs. We accepted. Moral to radicals: dress as you please but bring money.

In the warmth of Jack's *hors d'oeuvres*, Kemnitzer began talking about the people in the movement: "I was noticing in the library today that the biggest ass-holes were the social science majors. I have yet to meet a radical who knows about the arts, who is really literate, who can read a proper wine list." I gaped, then laughed. "Seriously," he continued, "I have yet to meet a radical who really knows how to be kind to somebody. Cleaver or Hayden, they're something else. I'm talking about students; it's a very strange thing when you begin to think your brothers on the left are your worst enemies. I've been in Berkeley for two years and I've never met a really healthy person. The left is unable to relate to other people."

Magid disagreed and suggested that there were plenty of radicals enjoying an active sex life.

"There's a difference between fucking and making love," said Kemnitzer. "There's a similarity in the process, but the distinction is in what's added to the process. In making love, there's commitment and the idea of intense belonging. But very few consider the left as an expression of themselves. What I'm trying to say is that nobody makes love to the movement."

Magid smiled and said, "I don't particularly think radicals are that different, or any more fucked up than the rest of society."

135

I agree with Larry. Student radicals don't seem to like each other much at most campuses. But fraternity brothers, nowadays, don't seem to like each other much, either. The radicals do enjoy talking about how unhappy they are. The fraternity brothers still wear the masks of the previous generation. The radicals exercise their discontent through impatience with the power structure. Other students repress their discontent and figure everything will be all right as soon as they inherit the power structure. But the power structure isn't so secure itself these days.

The radicals' impatience inspires another kind of behavior, too. By the time I reached Berkeley, I was calling it "Majorca or fight." I kept meeting students who posed these wild alternatives: "If we don't bring down the university this year, then I'm going to Majorca and paint." . . . "If we haven't radicalized this campus by the end of the quarter, then I'll accept the goddamn fellowship at Cambridge." Revolution or luxurious self-exile. *Now.* No wonder black militants don't trust the commitment of white radicals. Many white radicals are clever enough, wealthy enough and selfish enough to go to Majorca.

Such students refuse to believe that there's a less drastic choice, that there's truly room for them to participate in this society, that we would actively welcome their participation. One of the major troubles with students is that they're really afraid of being rejected even though they are the most knowing, most sophisticated, most vocal kids ever produced.

I left Berkeley thinking that the adult generation still offers advice or lip-service more often than it listens. Adults—whether parents or administrators—reject before they consider. The People's Park became a perfect example of such rejection.

I prefer to see students stay within our society. The carnival of Berkeley still offers an astonishing amount of intellectual excitement. The larger community still has an urgent need to shape itself a new middle before the next generation of troubled students is upon us. So we've got to open the system. We've talked about it enough.

David Graber, Class of '69—A Valedictory

The current student generation has an astonishing abundance of candor, curiosity, social concern, self-concern, impatience, verbal style and emotional confusion. David Graber, a 21-year-old Berkeley senior majoring in political theory, seems to have more of those qualities than most. Graber is a medium-bearded, well-bathed, occasionally-activist student who speaks for himself and sometimes for his generation.

The following is a condensation of a tape-recorded conversation. The sentences are David's although a few of the first names have been changed:

"My own flirtation with the SDS drives me crazy. I'll join every year, I'll go to meetings and I'll vote and I'll participate in things. Then I'll quit because the people start to sound like mewling complainers.

"Radicals are funny. The day before I saw you, I had lunch with Jerry. He starts telling me things like his grandfather was psychotic and locked up. And his father was psychotic. And his mother was psychotic and locked up. And yet there are Sociology Department studies showing radicals are also the healthiest people on campus.

"Well, now, Jerry's starting to wonder whether he's going to be psychotic. Then he switches the subject and starts saying, 'Next year, I think I'm gonna go to Oxford.' He's already been accepted at Oxford. And I said, 'Well then what's the point, if you're just gonna leave, you know. Is it a game?'

"And he said, 'When I'm really wrapped up in politics and there's something happening, I feel healthy and active and I'm enjoying life. And when I'm not, I'm miserable and I have to start worrying about personal problems.' The fact is, he has a hard time with girls and he's a sloppy sort of person and very lonely, I think. You know, his friends are political friends, which aren't the same as personal friends.

"SDS parties are not like the parties when my personal friends and I get together and we feel strong bonds of emotion and affection and love for one another. SDS parties are this intense interplay back and forth. The game, you know, who's the most radical? Who's gonna be a liberal tonight so we can jump on him? You either make a mistake and say something liberal or you do it on purpose because you're feeling nasty and want to fight back. And they'll jump on you. It's an exhausting thing. So I go in and then I pull out.

"Then I go in the woods and sit by brooks. This, other people do too—run away.

"The movement burns out its own. Mario Savio is an example. He's burned out. And people put him down, which hurts me. You know, they say he's out of it. Jerry said that. People are so impatient. I am too.

"I talked to Phil. And he tells me about when he was in his early 20s. He went down to the South and got busted for integrating lunch counters. And he said, 'What a gas.' He spent six days in jail and loved it. They sang and all that stuff. And then he told me about being in jail after the draft demonstration. And he said it was so somber. And he didn't particularly like most of the other guys in it. They irritated him. And yet he knew he was one of the Oakland Seven. He couldn't be Phil and the Oakland Six. So he's in it with them and he stuck it out. And he said, 'You know, it's changed. It's not the same. It's not a game anymore.'

"The Free Speech Movement, if you've ever heard tapes of the FSM, had singing. It was pretty happy and Joan Baez was there and all that sort of thing. If Nixon can't handle things psychologically, and loses his cool and starts shutting down—you know, he can get enough cops to repress this place. Or Reagan can. Then maybe there'll be a beat thing again, like the 50's when you couldn't buck McCarthy. They were all socialists but they didn't try, because it was useless.

"Maybe we're gonna retreat and gather together in dark little apartments and get stoned and sort of do our own thing and try to avoid contact with the baddies. But I'm irascible. I'm pugnacious and I like fighting. Pericles said in his funeral oration,

138

comparing Athens to Sparta, 'We do not say in Athens that those men who have no business in politics mind their own business. But rather we say that those men whose business is not politics have no business in Athens at all.' Every citizen has a debt and an obligation to get involved. And this is a dream, this participatory democracy thing, with anybody who's read any politics. Which is almost everybody at Cal . . .

"Are there old hippies? Are there any old alienated people? I don't know. Maybe this is the way we talk when we're young and it burns out, burns out of your soul. What happens to street people when they become 25 or 30? Do they eventually give up and get a job? Or do they hang on and become old street people? Sometimes this world is so insane. And Berkeley is so loony and alienated and miserable—you know, a cesspool of miserable people. But I don't know whether we want to be miserable or whether the attempt to be free makes us miserable. You know, my mother is always telling me, 'David, as you get older, things don't hurt as much.' And I keep thinking that what she's really saying is that you just lop off the tops and the bottoms. Life gradually dwindles off to some sort of a median.

"You know it's a crummy thing to settle for middleness, to settle for things somewhat better than your parents had. Like why is it I won't be satisfied being a teacher? I mean, I like teaching. I'm very pedagogic. I dig telling people things and having them react. I like lecturing. Why won't I settle for that? I know I won't . . .

"And yet I'm very aware that at Berkeley—despite the fact that friends deny this—radical movements are forever calling for faculty support. I think teachers are still father figures and authority figures, you know. 'For God's sake, please give us something to hold onto that's strong. Because if you don't tell us, things are gonna be much more chaotic and we really don't know where we are.'

"We really don't, you know. Like me, I'm monogamous. I'm essentially a kind of puritan. I don't like sleeping around. Maybe because I tried it and it didn't work, made me feel very uptight. For me, sex without real emotional caring was, you know, like masturbating over a body. Even this campus, despite the fact that there are supposed to be 1,100 unmarried couples living together, doesn't practice free love. It's not free love. You may change couples but it's always a couple. None of this, you know,

139

sleep with one girl Monday and one girl Tuesday. That isn't the way we operate. Because we are frightened. We *are* insecure.

"I still have a ridiculous sense of greatness. I want to be great, be unique. And when my roommate says, 'You're strange,' I enjoy being told that. I have a vision of myself swimming upstream. When we were talking about it, my roommate said he envisioned himself as a 'leaf afloat upon a stream of life.' And I said that bugs me. If anything, I'm a swimmer, choosing the point on either bank where I'm going to light. And I'm swimming against the current, you know, picking my own way. I may not know what I'm doing but I know there's nobody gonna tell me.

"Every once in a while when I'm in San Francisco—I love that town—and I pass all the businessmen and their highheeled secretaries, I get sad because there's no attachment, no ground zero for them. Nothing to hold onto. But when I retreat on my hikes, I say, 'Thank God, thank God.' Maybe that's why I'm such a conservation nut. Because I'm terrified of when there's no ground zero, nothing to hold onto.

"When I go into places in the city I enjoy, I'm very much aware of the underpinnings. There are so many times I feel like—boy, this is gonna be vain—feel like Christ in the temple, feel like swinging my fists and saying, 'You degenerate bastards. You're sick. You're loony.'

"Oh boy, what do we hold onto anymore? When I run off to Arizona or Utah or Mexico, what is it I hold onto? The soil? I crashed around the Southwest last spring—Arizona, New Mexico—you know, the home of the bigots and the brave. And I lost my mind.

"I was crying and feeling that red earth and saying, 'My God, I love this country. I really honestly love it.' And I am a patriot in my own perverted little way. And I don't want to leave. And I saw the Indians, you know, and they weren't friendly and I tried talking to them and they just weren't nice. But I understood why and I still love them. I remember coming back and telling my friends, 'I can't leave, I can't. I'm an American. I've been raised this way. I'm not a European. I'm not even a Canadian.'

"Even on the Southern California shore, I go crazy. With Hickel in for Secretary of Interior, I worry. You know what my reaction is? I would think of sending him threats. See? Here's the violence. Here's where the impatience is. But I'm not a violent person—I'm never gonna hurt him.

140

"But with Hickel, you know, his conservation crap, if we worry too much about water pollution, it's gonna interfere with industrial progress. Wow! Fuck you, Hickel. That kind of thing makes me want to send him some kind of crazy letter like one saying: 'You better produce three national parks next year, Hickel or else!' Completely crazy, I know. Did I tell you about my friend who phoned in a bomb threat to Howard Johnson's in L.A.? They emptied the whole place out. They never caught him, he called from a pay phone. But I know I could never do that, because all those people who were living in Howard Johnson's were the ones who really ate it. They had to charge out of their rooms and maybe some old lady could have had a heart attack.

"I couldn't do it. I'm too repressed."

EPILOGUE

Going back to college turned out to be an odyssey in myth removal, a learning experience that convinced me how inadequately our easy slogans and fragmentary battle reports reflect what is really happening on campuses.

I suppose it's only fair to admit that the press contributes to the myth-making problem. Media reporters tend to appear at a university only when something out of the ordinary is in process—riot, strike or sit-in—because the definition of news continues to be "that which is unusual."

The films of student violence and the descriptions of student protest *do* present a distorted picture of college life, primarily by omission. Even on a campus where a sit-in may have closed one major building, regular classes and regular scholarship are probably keeping 90 per cent of the students occupied. The gentlemen of the press—by training, habit and curiosity—concentrate on the troubles rather than the routines.

The presence of cameramen or reporters sometimes serves to make matters worse. Militants, especially militant students, feel an obligation to perform for the press once the press appears. The militants are sophisticated enough to know that newspapers and news programs feed on events in preference to discussion, on controversy more than consensus. The militants are not so sophisticated about predicting public response.

Their own excesses in rhetoric and action have often done injustice to their cause. Sometimes it's as if the activists were daring the media to record their words or print their pictures. So much has already been said about idealistic aims and noxious tactics that the ends-means arguments now enjoy their own stream of clichés. But it is true that many of the militants' methods have been either ill-planned or spontaneous—in effect, childlike screams for attention. Screams for media attention which, in turn, would call society's attention to a particular set of issues.

Society's attention has effectively been called, with predominantly hostile result. Polls indicate that the general public—more than administrators, more than politicians and certainly more than faculty members—is fed up with college unrest and in a mood to punish. Legitimate questions concerning campus governance, university defense contracts and minority recruitment have been obscurred for the public by "non-negotiable demands," nonsensical vandalism and Anglo-Saxon name calling.

Radical tactics have produced some extreme responses, such as the tear-gassing of the Berkeley campus and the shot-gunning on Berkeley streets in June of 1969. Excess has led to over-reaction which has caused further excess which could indeed stimulate the kind of repression that radicals keep predicting in their rhetoric. The mood to punish stimulates other tactics that also have unsalutary results. Every time outside force is applied to an internal campus disorder, a few moderate students convert to radicalism.

Radicals use repression as a recruiting tactic. And repressors use radicalism as an excuse to brutalize. That unholy relationship, between the masochists and the sadists, will have to be broken before sanity returns.

When I began the campus rounds, I did make an attempt to meet the so-called silent majority, those 90 per cent people who continue to go about college business as usual. They exist and they are approachable. But within their ranks live undergraduate creatures of almost every stripe: confirmed non-joiners, old-fashioned social climbers, new-model pacifists, tunnel-vision vocationalists, scholars, conformists and even a few silent anarchists. Between students on the new left and the hard right is a maze of a middle that doesn't function, practically or politically, as a majority. There are silent students but they have little effect on any shcool life outside their own. There is a non-activistic majority but the students in it are a mixed audience of spectators and not the major players.

The protagonists are on stage—activists from left or right—and they are the people who want to perform, who insist on participating. They make the drama and the noise . . . and the changes.

Radicals are surrounded by myths, most of which make the new left appear to be a stronger arm than it is.

143

I could find no persuasive evidence, for instance, that radical student groups are part of a shrewdly organized Communist conspiracy. Like the middle, there are too many different ideologies under the radical umbrella to sustain that notion. And there are too many conflicting nay-sayers involved to suggest the efficiency of Communism. At Berkeley, in particular, I learned that campus radicals are at constant war with each other and the national split within SDS during the summer of 1969 only confirms the disorganization of the movement.

It would be convenient to bill the Communists for college unrest because that makes an outside enemy accountable and removes some of our responsibility for the problem. The truth, however, is that campus radicals are quite American, definitely a part of each campus and clearly the sons and daughters of the middle class. They are inside agitators, which is one of the reasons they're so difficult to control or mollify. They are not alien nor so unlike their contemporaries in likes or life styles. Although they might not say so, most student radicals are different in degree and not in kind from their classmates.

Loyalty to a particular institution is an old myth. I found love of school apparent only at Stanford, Santa Cruz and Pomona. At the majority of campuses the reverse was almost the rule: the undergraduate fashion is to find fault with one's home college.

Nearly half of the students I met had already transferred schools at least once and a majority of the others had fairly definite plans to switch before their four undergraduate years were done.

The old football rivalries—the "big game" between USC and UCLA— have become far less important than political rivalries. Loyalty is within an academic discipline or an ideology now, replacing rah-rah and restrictive social clubs, crossing the boundaries of individual schools.

Loyalties have little to do with geography and a great deal to do with inter-campus movements.

Cheap jet fares are literally a motive part of the movement. A speaking circuit, not so unlike the old Chautauqua, thrives between California campuses. One radical can cover all the branches of the UC system within two or three days.

The inter-campus connections are especially strong among black students. The Black Students Union at almost every school maintains ties with BSUs at other campuses.

During the grim shut-down at San Francisco State, I remember hearing a rousing BSU spokesman named Jack Alexis threaten to instigate BSU strikes on all 18 state college campuses, sympathy strikes that would disrupt the entire system. At first, that sounded like more militant rhetoric. Before my travels were done I came to believe that such a statewide strike is not beyond possibility.

The black-imposed apartheid on most campuses is unhappy to see and unpleasant to contemplate. Black separatism on the outside is essentially a matter of polemics. At college, it is already in practice, especially among freshmen and sophomores.

Many black juniors and seniors began their higher educations in the older days, when a Negro was a noticeable but barely measurable fraction of the campus population. Those black students did make friends among whites and some of those friendships continue.

The black students who have come to colleges in the 1968-1969 years are different people. There are more of them and they were recruited. They were offered grants and inducements. They were primarily ghetto kids who grew up in a black society that had reason to distrust or fear whites.

This infusion of black students contained young people who were wholly unfamiliar with collegiate life styles, middle class mores or academic bureaucracy.

What they did know was their community and they went to school with strong ties to that community. It's not so surprising that the new black students stuck together and started complaining that institutions were not attuned to them nor attentive to their needs. The institutions weren't. Even with the best intentions, schools did not know how to address themselves to large numbers of non-middle class minority students. And the black newcomers didn't know how to adapt to the institutions without feeling disloyal to the community they came from, without seeming to run away and hide at a symbolically white ivory tower.

The shouts about black studies grew naturally out of the ignorance on both sides. There is a danger that a department of black studies might indeed increase anguish and apartheid on any campus. There is a counter-hope that by offering black students more of what they believe education should be about, institutions can at the same time begin to convince all students that college, at its best, is about the improvement of the entire human condition through cultivation of individual human potential.

145

The myth of the single cause—be it new left or nihilism, spoiled brats or militant blacks, impersonal professors or inept administrators, Vietnam war or even moral breakdown—does not stand up because any or all of the above may contribute to the troubles on a campus.

Present institutional unrest is not so unlike an individual suffering from insomnia. He may have a headache and a financial misery and a nagging wife and high blood pressure all at one time. Every one of his discomforts could keep him awake and each of them is likely to aggravate the other.

Removing one of the causes of campus unrest would alleviate the condition. The end of the war, for instance, would surely temper the radicalism that boils out of personal fear or humane principle. But a solution in Vietnam would not bring the schools back to ivy-covered apathy. Nothing will. That monotonous student word, relevance, is really an over-simple code name for a new kind of higher education, one that has to be in and of the world rather than detached from it.

Several scholars have traced the movement as it went from civil rights to peace mongering to the school grounds themselves. Having failed to save the South or Southeast Asia, students carried their complaints back on campus. School is familiar territory. And academicians are uniquely vulnerable to activism.

Young adults do believe that change is itself a constant of modern life. They understand the awesome speed of technology better than most of their elders. And part of their impatience is an attempt to keep up, personally, with the changes that whirl around them.

I know one student who is a sometime-radical, sometime-athlete, sometime-conservationist, sometime-girl chaser and sometime-scholar who earns excellent grades.

He thrashes into each of his activities with impartial excitement and dedication, rarely contradicting himself because everything he does leaps from a basic impatience. But an adult who saw this student shoving at police lines might have trouble recognizing him collecting sea shells along the coast. Just as the media normally observe a campus only when it's in the midst of a disturbance, most older people have a narrow-focus notion of what a demonstrator looks like.

One of the pleasures of being able to wander through the

colleges was meeting activists during their off hours, when they were behaving like other students. Only a tiny fraction of the militants are so absorbed by the movement as to be obsessed with it. The others do study and kiss girls and even write home to their parents. They are our kids and disowning them as freaks is not going to help them or us.

I confess that activists—left or right—usually impressed me with their brains, their alertness, their curiosity. And if I spent more time with them along the way than with non-activists, it was because they were generally more interesting, and I suppose because I share the journalistic understanding of news.

As the articles appeared in West Magazine, I began to receive mail from students, alums, parents and taxpayers. I separated parents from taxpayers because while all parents may think of themselves as harried taxpayers, many harried taxpayers do not think of themselves as parents.

Parental response was frequently sympathetic to student complaints, even when the elders felt confused or confuted by the activists' behavior.

Taxpayer response was predominantly outrage. Outrage at the indignities to institutions. Outrage at the ingratitude to the public system. Understandable outrage at the violence done to people. Disproportionate outrage at the damage done to property. The mood to punish was never clearer than in a letter from one taxpayer referring to the indiscriminate tear-gassing of the Berkeley campus by a National Guard helicopter: "I'd have gassed them twice as much, twice as soon," wrote the reader.

Alumni letters ran to form. If I seemed to have said nice things about their old school, alumni mail was warm and encouraging. If I seemed to be unkindly critical, then the mail was somewhat choleric. Alums are still loyal. In the case of USC, nearly 95 per cent of the alumni respondents thought I had been unduly harsh toward their alma mater. Interestingly, more than half of the letters from USC students said that the article had been too easy on their school. When I told some of the infuriated alums that undergraduates did not share their opinion, the alums snorted and claimed that only radicals would sit down and write letters to the media. Maybe so.

No adults have yet devised a blueprint for keeping campuses

147

calm. After the bloody school year of 1968-69, several schools established summer task forces to devise tactics that would protect a campus at something less than point of bayonet.

I don't pretend to have any disruption-proof notions but there are practices I would advocate: First, I'd avoid calling outside troops or police on campus unless the danger of real physical harm—to people—was clear and present. If police did have to be called, I'd ask them not to make arrests on campus during the disturbance. Names can be taken, militants can be re-routed without dragging students across the quad to a paddy wagon. Riots have been enflamed when police handcuffed and hauled off student militants. The presence of police at a school triggers too many automatic responses. A large number of students—including members of the "silent majority"—recognize police as billy clubs in uniform and not as human beings. A large number of police look at long hair as a sure symptom of revolution. As long as kids and cops persist in seeing each other as natural enemies, they should be prevented from meeting during a disturbance if at all possible.

Student referenda, taken *prior* to a disturbance help prevent disturbance. Student-faculty participation in the campus' own internal security force also helps. And student access to the administration, to the boggling machinery that runs the school, is essential.

As sad as the 1968-69 season was, there were some lessons amidst disturbances. One of the ironies of San Francisco State was that many of the striking students learned more about politics, public address, group dynamics and psychology outside the classrooms than they would have inside the classrooms.

Such education is too dangerous and too expensive to advocate but it did take place.

I have some hope and some hunch that the miseries of 1968-69 may spawn a rebirth of non-violent protest. The application of tactics from Jesus or Ghandi or King did not work the first time around college campuses in the mid-60's. Activists, because of their impatience, quickly came to believe that exemplary behavior or passive resistance were too tame to move administration mountains. So radicals dropped lofty tactics as they raised demands; violence, supposedly in the pursuit of virtue, became acceptable. "By any means necessary," became a fashionable slogan.

Violence did not work, however, in 1968-69. It produced arrests, explosions, opened skulls, deaths and repression but hardly any advances in the pursuit of virtue. Now that violence has proved it merely begets more violence, the time for a reassertion of exemplary protest may be here. Students, whose sense of history is not nearly as strong as their sense of injustice, had to see for themselves that violence hardens mens' minds instead of changing them.

At the same time, I'm concerned about the next few years at high schools—not so much because the SDS has threatened to organize secondary students, but because other aspects of ferment have already moved down through the grades. Drug use moved from the college crowd to the high school set and down to the junior highs, changing emphasis along the way from an experiment in self-awareness to a pitiable exercise in escape.

The peace movement also worked its way down from colleges to high schools to junior highs. And now the cry for participation in matters of expression and curriculum is already activating high school students.

Oddly, high schools may be the most change-resistant institutions in the educational system and hence the most ripe for activists' complaints. The reforms in schooling have mainly happened at top and bottom—in the universities and in the elementary grades—leaving secondary schools in the middle but behind times. Elementary school changes—in curriculum and individual counseling—have produced a generation of high schoolers who resist dress codes or censoring of student speeches. Meanwhile, these same kids have watched their older brothers and sisters operate and participate at colleges

High school activism may well be more unsophisticated and potentially more destructive than university activism, attracting many students who are more interested in raising hell than social issues. High school activism is also likely to produce faster, tougher administrative response, with police becoming an adjunctive part of the public school system.

The most effective way to prevent serious disturbances at the secondary level is by introducing change, by inviting high schoolers to understand the operation of their campuses, by recognizing that 10th graders do have a stake in citizenship. We can't teach responsibility without giving youngsters a chance to practice responsibility.

I left the college circuit liking students, enjoying their candor

149

and social committment, admiring how much they already knew—and worrying about how much they didn't know they didn't know.

A campus is still the best place to teach someone how much he doesn't know and a school is probably still the best setting for a person to find his own sense of purpose.

There are still joys in being young and being educated.

I found a joy in being around, watching.